Lands of the Unexpected
Memoirs of the Middle East 1930-1960
Ezra Young

❊The Sunstone Press
Santa Fe, New Mexico USA

FIRST EDITION

Book Design: Douglas Jerrold Houston
Cover: From a painting by Ali Sami Boyar. This Shadirvan ("Fountain of Ablutions") is in the courtyard of Ayasofya Mosque in Istanbul. The fountain was built in honor of Sultan Mahmoud the First.

Brief sections reprinted by permission of Charles Scribner's Sons from "Turkey, Old and New" by Selma Ekrem, Copyright 1947 Selma Ekrem. Other excerpts reprinted by permission from "History of the Arabs" by Philip K. Hitti, St. Martin's Press, Inc., Macmillan & Co., Ltd.; from "Suleiman The Magnificent" by Harold Lamb, Copyright 1951 by Harold Lamb, Doubleday & Company, Inc.; from "Arab Unity, Hope and Fulfilment" by Fayez A. Sayegh, Devin-Adair Company, Old Greenwich, Conn.; and from "The Arab World" by Nejla Izzeddin, Henry Regnery Co., Chicago.

Library of Congress Cataloging in Publication Data

Young, Ezra.
   Lands of the unexpected.

   Bibliography: p.
   1. Near East--Description and travel. 2. Turkey--Description and travel. 3. Young, Ezra. 4. Young Men's Christian Associations--Biography. I. Title.
DS49.7.Y68   956'.04   78-75083
ISBN O-913270-77-6

Published in 1979 by The Sunstone Press
Post Office Box 2321, Santa Fe, New Mexico 87501

CONTENTS

ACKNOWLEDGEMENTS TO:

Ali Sami Boyar, Turkish painter, and onetime Curator of Ayasofya Museum, appreciation for use of cover material, and for his friendship.

John Brewer, Houston, Texas, appreciation for photograph on back cover.

Herman Kreider, James Clark and **Ezra Young,** credit and thanks for photographs in the text.

Esther Keating and **Clarence Noyce,** thanks for the loan of Middle Eastern slides.

Barbara Hoon for her comments and excellent typing of the manuscript.

James Clois Smith, Jr., Douglas Jerrold Houston, and **Melissa H. Engestrom** at The Sunstone Press for their encouragement and services beyond expectation, our thanks.

Jessamine, for patience, encouragement and correction of grammar.

Gertrude Reynolds, for her encouragement and support.

David, Maja and **Barbara Young** for reading the manuscript and comments.

Earl and **Mabel Brehm** for reading manuscript and suggestions.

Pat Kailer, for a writer's suggestions.

Garnet Guild (Quaker, and onetime teacher in Friends' School, Ramallah, Jordan); **Frank Kiehne** and **Harry Brunger** (YMCA); **Paul** and **Anna Limbert, Paul** and **Margaret Anderson** (former YMCA Executives); **Margaret Blemker,** (United Church of Christ—World Ministries); **Harry** and **Virginia Howard** (formerly with American Embassy in Beirut). Special thanks for reading manuscript and for constructive criticism.

FOREWORD

David Finnie has reminded us in his "Pioneers East" that Americans generally have forgotten — if indeed, they ever knew — the long past in the relationship between the United States and the Ottoman Empire, or between the American people and the varied and gifted people in the Middle East. Yet American missionaries and educators began going to the Ottoman Empire at the very beginning of the nineteenth century. They left an enduring legacy in the establishment of Robert College (1863), the American University in Cairo (1920), Aleppo College and Athens College, to mention only a few of the better known institutions in the Middle East. As late as World War II, knowledge of the people of the Middle East was meager. Two groups of Americans had had experience among the Muslims — the missionaries and the teachers, and the managers of airlines and oil companies.

Ezra Young, whom I first met in Beirut in the Fall of 1957, fits into the American tradition in the Middle East and spent some 20 years in that much troubled area — 15 of them in the Turkish Republic — following an invitation from the Turkish Dershane (School) Board and the International Committee of the YMCA to serve in Turkey. Because of World War II, he preceded his wife, Jessamine, by almost two years. The Dershane program included a language and commercial school, sports and gym program, dormitory and summer camp.

During his 20 years in the Middle East, Ezra Young's major assignments included four years in Adana, Turkey, as a social worker and playground supervisor for the American Board Mission; as Fraternal Secretary of the Dershane in Istanbul; and as Fraternal Secretary to the Lebanese YMCAs. In addition, he did volunteer work with the Palestinian refugees through UNRWA. He was co-chairman of the Near East Christian Council Committee for Refugee Work; and assisted the World Alliance of YMCAs in their establishment of a training center for social and recreational youth leaders among the Palestinian refugees. He also served as advisor in a training center for young YMCA secretaries from Egypt, Iraq, Jordan, Gaza and Lebanon, and was co-chairman of The Lebanon Emergency Committee, serving 30,000 victims of the 1958 turmoil in Lebanon.

Ezra Young's memoirs do not deal primarily in politics or even history, except insofar as necessary to place his own life and work in the Middle East in appropriate context. Rather, his memoirs are an account of the efforts of a man and his wife to share experiences and to be helpful during an especially difficult and troublesome period in Turkey and the Arab World. The memoirs should be widely read and studied. Careful consideration should lead to a deeper understanding of other people who grew up in a different culture, and it might even prove helpful in their (the people of the area) making adjustments to an ever-changing world.

Harry N. Howard

Middle East Institute
Washington, D.C.

Former Diplomat, American Embassy, Beirut, Lebanon
Former Professor, George Washington University
Participant in the United Nations Founding at San Francisco — 1940's
Author, recognized authority on the Middle East, Member of the King-Crane Commission

ii

To Jessamine, Maja, David and Barbara Young
who first suggested these Memoirs;

To our dear Grandson, David,
that he may become a man
worthy of his times; and

To scores of others at home
and in the Middle East
who have made these Memoirs possible.

In Loving Appreciation

PREFACE

In 1930, during my first assignment in Turkey, a wise old Cypriot philosopher said to me, "Just remember that you are working in a region where the unexpected is normal." In the more than 20 years that followed, this became increasingly evident; the more one stays in that part of the world the less one dares to predict. An American missionary, with 30 years service in various lands of the region once commented, "I can say that I have never been bored, for each morning as the Muezzin calls the faithful to prayer I wonder what new surprise or excitement the day will bring."

Given the uncertainty, and the unpredictable nature of life and events in that part of the world, this book will not pretend to be a political treatise, lest these thoughts become irrelevant and obsolete. Rather it is intended to be an inside look at personal and human relations as experienced by the writer, his colleagues, his family and friends over two decades.

Significant to the psychology and moods of these lands is a legend about the camel which compensates him for an often burdensome life. The legend goes: "Among our people the 'tespih' (string of 33 prayer beads) is told three times by the faithful Muslims to name the 99 names of Allah. But only the camel knows the 100th name of Allah. Hence his proud, and aloof, mien." In lands where fantasy and fact often mingle, it is not difficult to believe the legend of the camel.

The following tales of Turkey and the Middle East are like a string of 33 beads (plus one) held together by memory. They reflect the humor and wisdom, as well as the life-style, aspirations and hopes of the people of these volatile and fascinating countries. If the reader completes these Memoirs with a fresh understanding of the people and events in this vitally important part of the world, the writer will be richly rewarded for the years of experience and study which have gone into the writing of "Lands of the Unexpected."

I apologize to Turkish linguists for not using the extra letters in the Turkish alphabet but only the phoneticized sounds.

Albuquerque, New Mexico
1979

iv

THE INFIDEL'S DONKEY

It had been a long day, and the summer sun of 1946 boiled around our Army Jeep even though it was six in the evening. All afternoon we had driven east from Ankara (Turkey's capital) through dust-filled winds, pushing 200 miles into ancient Asia Minor to reach the welcomed coolness of Amasya at the foot of the Black Sea mountain ranges. Around a sharp curve we began to traverse a narrow canyon, cooled by giant poplars on one side of the highway, and flanked by lush rice fields on the other. What a contrast to the semi-sophistication of the capital where we had been entertained the evening before at a cocktail party, a sendoff for what most people thought a dangerous journey in the "unknown lands" of the East. One friend remarked gloomily, "What is there to see or do in those wild lands of central and eastern Turkey?"

Tommy (Lewis Thomas) my Jeep companion, an orientalist from Princeton, then teaching at Robert College in Istanbul, and I decided to spend our holidays visiting some remote towns and cities in northern and western Turkey. We were semi-camping; Tommy knew classical Turkish and I knew the idiomatic Turkish so we felt completely at home on this vast plain of Anatolia (the Turkish interior). Moreover, we knew that when we arrived in Amasya we would find a small hotel and a fabulous restaurant where, according to custom, you were invited to the kitchen to choose your own Shish Kebab, salad, pahlava (a sweet, syrupy pastry laced with sliced apples, the piece-de-resistance of the town) and strong, strong Turkish coffee. The apples of Amasya are unbelievably large and sweet; they are served as a delicacy on tables of the Middle East just as the equally delicious mountain-grown apples of Lebanon are flown to Europe (Rome, Paris, Berlin and London) to grace the menus of the great restaurants of that continent.

As we coasted down a long hill between fragrant trees laden with apple blossoms, a tall, ornate minaret of the town's Mosque came into view. And suddenly the curious, and inevitable, crowd of youngsters came to welcome us and our strange craft. In Turkish they were shouting, "Bak sana, gowerin eshegi geliyor" ("Look, the infidel's donkey is coming"). No offense was meant in calling us infidels; it was just their way of welcome. Their delight, and smiles, belied any unfriendliness. We, too, forgot everything we had planned and took the children two-by-two for rides in our "donkey." That night we were the "toast of Amasya" and had little sleep for the word spread until almost everyone in town, young and old, had a ride they would not soon forget. We never arrived at our hotel but were entertained in the home of the Muhtar (mayor of the village). Next morning, bleary-eyed but happy, we discovered the Jeep, neat as a pin and filled with gasoline, a scarce commodity in that town. It was their way of saying "lutfen gene buyurunuz" ("come again, please"). (Our review of the Ottoman cities deserves a special chapter later in this book.)

The "donkey" served us well for four more years, and was then sold for $100 more than when it was bought earlier as war surplus in Paris. Three years later we graduated to a Jeepster but our daughter, five years old at the time, and our teenaged son missed the ubiquitous Jeep. Driving from Ankara to Istanbul (some 300 miles) my son Dave and I spent the night in an old Inn, or Caravan Saray, in rugged and remote mountains. At bedtime we heard a noisy clatter and loud voices in the village square under our window. Around an ancient Jeep a crowd had gathered and all were giving advice to a grimy mechanic who had managed to get himself headfirst beside the motor with only his feet sticking out over the radiator. Dave took one look at the immobilized vehicle and said, "Dad, I would swear that's our old Jeep and if it is, I can start it with a hammer." A mammoth hammer was produced from a truck nearby and my son climbed in beside the mechanic with only his feet sticking out. He made the most of his moment. With a mighty swing he lifted the hammer and struck the side of the motor. To everybody's amazement, the old motor coughed twice, and started. The crowd shouted, "Mashallah" ("what a miracle Allah has wrought") and "Chocuk usta" ("the child is a genius").

Thanks to Dave and his ingenuity, the town was ours. Candy, sticky ice cream, flat bread and yogurt were produced. The owner of the Jeep gave his blessing and the Muhtar made it official. (Why spoil it all by telling the crowd that the Jeep had been ours and had been started frequently with a hammer blow?) That was 1952. Somewhere, somehow, we believe our "infidel's donkey" is still serving a purpose because it truly seemed immortal and indestructible. Even now, after 25 years, we have a special feeling for that endearing and incredible machine.

A Crusader's castle
in the Taurus Mountains, Turkey in 1931.

KEMAL ATATURK
EMANCIPATOR OF TURKEY

Following World War I, Turkey, "The Sick Man of Europe," was defeated, divided, broken, occupied by foreign powers, and scorned by the Allies. It was ripe for a change and for leadership the people could respect and follow. They hungered for a hero and a strong leader. Mustafa Kemal Pasha, fresh from a victory over the British at Gallipoli in the Dardanelles (ancient Hellespont, Turkish "Chanak Kale" or "Boaz Ichi") was that man. But the Sultan, Abdul Hamit, who feared and envied Kemal's popularity had other plans for the charismatic young Officer; he gave orders that "Capt. Kemal" be sent into Eastern Turkey as Inspector of the First Army, hoping that the people would forget him. Little did the Sultan, sulking in his comfortable "Saray" (palace) at Constantinople and surrounded by fawning followers, realize that this would be the beginning rather than the end of Kemal's career. Instead, the rise of Kemal as a popular leader of the revolt against the Sultan and the occupying powers (Britain, France, Italy and Greece) was very rapid. The young leader used his power and influence well in Samsun on the Southern Coast of the Black Sea where the 1923 Revolution was born and from where it was launched. In a brief time the Sultan was banished from Constantinople and the occupying powers left Turkey in disarray. However, the war dragged on for several years before the revolutionary government could be established. During this time the Turkish and Greek forces (the latter occupying "Izmir," or "Smyrna") were in deadly combat. The war seesawed back and forth until the capture of Smyrna by the Turkish armies; there was much suffering on both sides during the conflict but after the war there was a humane exchange of populations which permitted the Greeks to return to Greece and the Turks in Greece to migrate to Turkey. Allied shipping assisted in the exchange. Also a YMCA Secretary then working in Smyrna, helped with the complexities. A prominent Turkish doctor, Ramzi Gonench, who later served in the American Hospital in Adana and as Head of the Red Crescent Society, was honored by the British Empire for his services during this humane and historic occasion.

In a masterly campaign and strategy, Kemal Pasha marched at the head of his army from Samsun to Smyrna, then to a swampland near the ancient city of Ankara where he decreed that this site, so unpromising then, would be the place for the new capital of Turkey, for he wished to disassociate the new Republic from the old capital in Constantinople. He then renamed the city "Istanbul" or "Istambol." Thus Turkey gradually ceased to be "the Sick Man of Europe," rising from its long lethargy with new pride and hope, to become a sovereign Nation. Meanwhile, in a final gesture of defiance the Sultanate condemned Mustafa Kemal Pasha to death in absentia, and Soviet Russia, for many years an enemy of Turkey, became the first country to recognize the revolutionary government of Ataturk.

Several factions which made up the revolution were unique. Perhaps Kemal Pasha was the only commander who could weld them into a fighting force. The elements included the peasants from Anatolia who had the least to lose and perhaps the most to gain, dissident officers from the Sultanata, disenchanted youth, young officers loyal to Kemal Pasha who had fought beside him at Gallipoli, and those wonderful women who longed for freedom and the franchise promised to them by Kemal Pasha. Defying ancient traditions and custom and discarding their veils (those symbols of submission, servitude and discrimination), they joined the men of the revolution, sharing the hardship and the hope.

It was during the revolution that Halide Edip Hanim, and her husband, Adnan Adavar joined forces with Ataturk. These distinguished intellectuals became valued leaders of the new Republic. Halide Edip Adavar became famous throughout the globe for her writing, lectures and interpretation of the new Turkey. She was an effective leader in the emancipation of Muslim women. For a time this great Turkish patriot and Ataturk had their political differences, but her admiration for his genius never faltered. Like Kemal Ataturk, Halide Edip was sentenced to death in absentia.

The revolution was a leveler, especially between officers and footsoldiers, for under the Sultans there was a very clear caste system. Ataturk (called Father Turk by his people; also Gazi, or Conqueror) soon began to change even the military traditions, giving new dignity and worth to the average soldier.

For example, when I first went to Turkey in 1930, I remember a pitiful scene of a ragged Turkish "mehmetcik" (foot-soldier) pushing a baby-buggy through the park behind a nattily dressed officer and his wife. Scenes like this disappeared as Ataturk's reforms became effective.

After the battles ended and the task of forming a new government began, Ataturk said, "Give us ten years of peace to build our Nation." This was a rallying cry that united the people and won the respect of many nations. Henceforth, with lightning speed Ataturk's new government instituted reforms such as the Italian Penal Code and the Swiss Civil Code, replacing the "Sheriyat" or religious laws which had served their time and were no longer suited to new needs. Meanwhile, the President, who had resigned from his Army command and had become a civilian so he could rebuild his beloved Turkey, imported skilled linguists from Hungary and other nations to change the alphabet so the written language could become phonetisized (using the Latin alphabet and four Turkishized letters) to replace the ancient Arabic script. The President of Turkey was not satisfied to remain in the capital and give orders for these revolutionary reforms. He vigorously toured the towns and villages demonstrating the new writing in schools and coffee-houses. Also, he took the bold step, not popular with the conservative religious leaders of substituting Western headgear for the Fez. If Ataturk had not set the example by wearing a Western hat on his tours, giving impetus to this sweeping reform, the Fez might have stayed as a religious symbol.

Whether it is fact or fantasy one will never know, but a smart merchant in New York is alleged to have heard of the new-style headgear and made a fortune with a shipment of hats and caps to Turkey. To the surprise of many foreigners living in Turkey in the twenties, the changeover from Fez to hat or cap was almost total.

Perhaps one of the most radical reforms took place in Ankara at an Inaugural Ball soon after the government was formed. Ataturk invited all of his new deputies elected to the government to attend the ball, with their wives unveiled. It was a command performance, so who could say "no" to Ataturk, the Gazi! Ataturk himself again set the example by dancing with almost every woman in the ballroom. A Turkish Army friend told us years later that perhaps no one but Ataturk could have gotten away with it. A new alphabet, new codes of law, new headgear and new social customs, all within a few years, could only be achieved by leaders with courage and possessed of vision and a dream, but down-to-earth and sincere in their love for their nation and their people.

A part of the greatness of Ataturk was his statement on the eve of the formation of the new government, "No one personality could have inspired, or achieved, these remarkable changes. And our wonderful people, out of their love of justice and their desire for freedom, played their part." Ismet Inonu, the Prime Minister, was Ataturk's righthand man throughout the changes; in 1937, when Ataturk died, Inonu became the second President of the Republic.

So this near-miracle, a new Turkey, was born in 1923. Still untried and relatively unknown, Turkey, unfettered by its past and hopeful about its future, was ready to take its place with dignity among the nations. It was a distinguished American diplomat, Admiral Bristol, who believed in this new nation and urged the American government to recognize Turkey as a sovereign nation. The Admiral's trust will never be forgotten by the Turks. That America and Turkey had always been friends, even when during World War I they were for a time on opposite sides, was no doubt a factor in this recognition. It has been quite remarkable that during all of the troubles in the Middle East and elsewhere that the American Schools in that region remained open almost all of the time.

Among so many memories of Turkey one stands out. It was during a reception in Istanbul where I met Ataturk. One never forgot those penetrating eyes, nor the masterful manner of a really great man. After my introduction by a Turkish friend, the President said, "I understand that you are working with our youth through the American Mission in Adana — social and playground work, I believe. As you know our Government places a high priority on anything constructive for our young people. We thank you and welcome you to Turkey." To a young man newly arrived and knowing only 200 works of Turkish the concern and friendliness of Ataturk were tremendously impressive. Through an interpreter I informed the President that credit for the playground and social work should be given to the originator of the project, Miss Lillian Brauer, a missionary of the American Board in Adana, and to our Turkish teachers who were doing a wonderful service.

Whatever may have been the personal foibles of Ataturk, here for the first time in Turkey was a leader with magnetism and an incorruptible public integrity. A mark of his foresight and his genius is that many years after his passing, this beloved leader's reforms and influence remain a strong current in Turkish life and in the Turkish nation, as well as in neighboring nations.

Ataturk and his colleagues in the government kept two aims constantly before the people: opposition to expansion of Turkey beyond its borders and a desire to make Turkey self-sufficient and progressive with a Western slant, but keeping basic goals. The potentials to fulfill these aims are in the country and the people.

THE ART OF DICHOTOMY

DICHOTOMY: "A division, or the process of dividing into two mutually exclusive or contradictory groups."

Webster's Dictionary

One trait, or behavior pattern, that often confuses the Western mind is the practice of dichotomy in the Middle East. In recent history we have seen this tendency dramatized by President Anwar Sadat of Egypt and Prime Minister Manachem Begin of Israel during the Summit at Camp David in 1978 and in their private and public announcements. Dichotomy in the pronouncements of Middle Eastern leaders is almost universal. They have one method or mood in public statements and another in private, unofficial statements. Unless the foreigner sorts these out, he can easily become confused about policies and misjudge the motives of the leaders. This is why it seems to old hands in the Middle East that it was very wise to conduct negotiations in secret, and one would hope that future negotiations can be carried on in this manner.

In the idiom of the American Indian, this dichotomy is aptly described as "speaking with forked tongue." Once the newcomer has accepted this behavior as normal among the leaders of the Middle Eastern nations, he is more likely to be understood and welcomed. And, it is also necessary to know the various languages in order to effectively communicate in Turkey, or the Arab countries.

During the several times of official tension between the U.S. government and the government of Turkey over the Cyprus issue we found little personal hostility toward us as individual Americans, but there were some bitter feelings among the Turks that the U.S. Government had taken a position favoring the Greek majority in Cyprus over the Turkish minority, even behaving as if the Turks had few rights because they were a minority. In Turkey there were speeches in the Parliament, demonstrations in the streets and even attacks against American Government buildings. Two United States Information Services libraries were attacked and even non-government buildings like the "Amerikan Dershane" (former YMCA; from this point on "Dershane" will be used instead of YMCA) were threatened. One evening when the demonstrations were at their height, we saw some students from the Dershane joining the crowd in shouting and threats. That same evening some university students who had been in the demonstration came and apologized, saying: "This was not against you personally."

Some visitors, as well as persons assigned to Turkey, make the mistake of assuming that the rhetoric of the people they meet and their actions are one. Those of us who have lived and worked for many years there are astonished at what we used to call "the forty-eight hour experts" who thought they knew more than we did. In fact, the longer we stayed on the scene the less we thought we knew about some matters. Very often the glibness and charm of the people in dealing with these short-stayers seemed a cover-up for real feelings. Lest one be too hasty in accusing the people of being insincere, this behavior is thoroughly justified when it is understood that for many centuries these people have been exploited by foreigners, and some of their own countrymen. Once the Turks are convinced that your rhetoric is in harmony with your intentions, you will find them responding in kind.

During a summer cruise stop in Istanbul in 1946, several American friends dropped in to visit us in our home. We had invited some Turkish friends in for tea to meet them. One Turk, so astonished at the warmth between our visitors and us, remarked, "You must have known these people a long time to be so friendly." "As a matter of fact," we replied, "we have known them less than a year." With utmost tact the Turkish friend said, "We have a saying in our country: no one is your friend until he has eaten your bread and walked in your shoes.!" And he added, "In the old days when two caravans were about to meet, the strongest, wisest men in each caravan were sent out as 'advance men' to size up the other caravan. We proceed on the basis that every man is your enemy until proven otherwise; you reverse this by assuming that every man is your friend until proven differently." Therefore, it is not surprising that we Americans, and Westerners in general, are considered to be very naive in our human relations.

Once you accept this dichotomy even with some of the simplest of persons, you learn to live with it and to be realistic about it. For example, while I was in Turkey, my father, back in Pennsylvania, became critically ill. The family sent me a cable which my staff kept from me for two weeks, and when another cable followed, announcing his death, they kept this news from me for a week. They simply do not like to deliver bad news. To them this is customary, rather than cruel, but one never quite adjusts to it.

The art of dichotomy has also helped a country like Turkey in its foreign affairs. After World War I, when the Allied victors met to consider peace, they did so partly in revenge, and partly for constructive reasons. However, in the case of Turkey they were prepared to punish her for siding with Germany during the war. So little knowledge, or understanding did the Prime Ministers of Britain, France and Italy have of the true pride and mind of the Turks, that they were inclined to hold them in line through a policy of occupation; thence they decided to carve up Turkey and establish zones throughout the country, promptly writing off the Turks as a nation. Of course they had not reckoned with Ataturk, mentioned previously, who in short order tossed out the Sultan and the occupying powers to form a Republic.

As a "second-rate enemy" (the words are those of one of the Allied negotiators) Turkey was nevertheless asked to send representatives to Lausanne to present their case. Ismet Inonu Pasha was the leader of the delegation representing Turkey. Lloyd George of Britain tried through an interpreter to explain to the Turkish Prime Minister just what the status of his country would be. Following a long explanation, Ismet Pasha turned to Lloyd George remarking in French, "Mr. Prime Minister, would you repeat that statement please, for I am deaf." Later negotiators dealing with the astute and intelligent Ataturk, remarked in utter frustration, "Most of the top men we dealt with followed the pattern set by Ismet Inonu declaring that they, too, were deaf." Finally a Western diplomat assigned to Ankara summed it all up in an unforgettable one-liner, "In the new Turkish Government at Ankara everybody seems to be deaf except Ataturk and they made him President."

On such trivialities sometimes hang the fate of nations. American Ambassador Grew, a career diplomat widely respected in Turkey, once said that "everyone should have a healthy respect for Ataturk as an accomplished diplomat." I believe that Ataturk could return the compliment.

One never knew when Ataturk would choose to negotiate without notice. In fact, one of his favorite times for diplomacy would be the wee hours of morning during a card game, especially with the American and Belgian Ambassadors present. No one in this spot would ever underestimate the Turks.

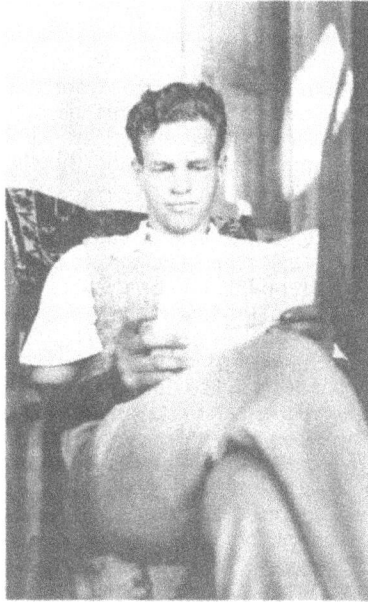

The author, at age 30, some 18 months after arriving in Adana, Turkey in 1932.

ALEPPO
CROSSROADS OF THE MIDDLE EAST

In a narrow, cobbled street of Aleppo, Syria, one can still see a bilingual sign in Arabic and French indicating that this is a camel caravan route. To prove it there is a crude drawing of a camel with an arrow toward the East. The camel sign is out of character with the larger sign for Coca Cola down the street. The ancient sign is a dramatic symbol of Aleppo's onetime importance as a center for trade and commerce. For centuries past the camel caravans, winding across the desert from Bagdad and beyond, brought spices and tea from India and China, dates from Bagdad, china from the Far East, silk and cotton cloth from the East, rare rugs from Persia and precious gems from storied places enroute. Returning caravans from the West opened up the ancient cities of the East with small machines, tools and the myriad products from the West. History records that as many as 25 caravans a day would enter Aleppo from East and West. It was only with the opening of the Suez Canal, and of other trade routes through India and the Mediterranean, that the number of caravans dwindled to a trickle.

The significant French influence during the years that Syria was under French Mandate had its effect on westernizing this ancient land. Then, too, following the First World War when Turkey became a Republic under Ataturk, Syria, the southern neighbor of Turkey, was shaken by the far-reaching reforms of her neighbor to the North. The coming of the railroad, the Orient Express, linking Berlin to Bagdad also opened up both East and West to Syria.

However, customs and mentality entrenched over the centuries in the Muslim Religion change very gradually, so even in recent years one still finds remnants of the old beliefs and culture, especially in the covered bazaar. An occasional veiled woman may still be seen, making her way shyly through the bazaar, in a world still largely dominated by men. But she is an exception to many women, smartly dressed and from more permissive backgrounds. Also one may see among the men dressed in business suits, a stately patriarch in long white "burnooz" (gown), and wearing a red Fez with decorated band indicating that he has made the "Haj"(pilgrimage to Mecca.) One young Arab we talked with was incensed that we took photos of old Aleppo rather than the new, but he was placated when we photographed him in front of a modern soda fountain!

In the 1930's my friend from Robert College on the Bosphorus (the former American College) and I decided to spend a holiday in Aleppo with Arab friends. For two weeks we explored the old and the new in Aleppo. Herman Kreider, a superb photographer, and a scholar and writer in Turkish, found the covered bazaar with its small shops, Mosques, Caravan Sarays, coffeeshops and people, fascinating and tempting for his camera. As long as we took photos of the people, they permitted us to snap almost anything except their wives. One evening after a five-course feast in our Syrian hosts' garden, he said sadly, "If Allah does not intervene, it will be only a few more years before what you have seen in the bazaar will change so you should take photos and make notes now." That was the nudge that we needed to write about and to photograph Aleppo. Back in the USA three years later, our story, amply photographed, appeared in the old "Travel Magazine."

As one lingers in a sidewalk coffeeshop, sipping the strong, twice-boiled brew, one is reminded that the old order is passing, with Cadillacs instead of caravans, Coca Cola instead of native lemonade, and very loud Western Jazz drowning out even the sometimes louder Arab music. (However, we agreed that the lyrics in Arabic seemed less repetitive and more interesting than the limited lyrics of some Western jazz.) As an undercurrent to the East-West music there was always the "tric-track" of the backgammon checkers and the contented hum of the hubble-bubble pipes, which we called the first filter!

From our favorite coffeeshop we could see the massive Citadel, historical center-piece of the city, which has withstood five invasions, including one by Tamerlane in 1401. But most of all we enjoyed the people, one of whom induced me to smoke the hubble-bubble or "Nargillah." Fortunately, our benefactor did not see me an hour later when I lost all of a very full Arab lunch as a result of my smoking. Then and there, I decided that so far as the "hubble-bubble" was concerned, they could have it.

As the reader may know, one of the delightful indoor sports in the Middle East is bargaining. The merchant, sitting cross-legged in his emporium, dreamily smoking his Nargillah is inscrutable and seemingly indifferent to the passing parade. But do not let him deceive you; for he is ready to trade at the drop of a Piaster. One never begins with bargaining, but with an herbal tea, part of the hospitality of every shopkeeper. Then you pass the time of day, discussing everything except why you came, just as if he were not the merchant, and you were not the customer. Moreover, you must never admire anything in the shop, for custom says that the shopkeeper must then give what you admired to you as a gift. It is uncanny how they know your psychology before you know theirs, and how shrewd they are in reading your intentions. Since bargaining is "the name of the game" for they would rather bargain and sell for less, than make more without bargaining.

Before we left Istanbul for Syria an Arab friend said, "You have not seen Aleppo until you tour the Suk Cuma (Friday market). We found it fascinating, for it is the combination of Flea Market, open-air restaurant, country fair and old-home week. The most unusual experience is to be in the open-air restaurant where cooks bend over their small "mangals," charcoal fires, preparing flat fried bread; shish kebab (made of lamb, not beef); "patlican dolma" (eggplant stuffed with rice, pine nuts and small bits of meat); and "baklava." Top this off with a small cup of Syrian coffee, it is a "moveable feast," no less. Compared with this cuisine, most Shish Kebabs in America are a pale, and soggy copy of the original. Exceptions are to be found at restaurants run by Armenians, Arabs or Turks on Lexington Avenue in New York City, and some other American cities. If you are squeamish about the varied odors in the streets and their effect, it would be advisable to have some Bromo Seltzer in pocket when you eat in a covered bazaar.

If you were blindfolded and taken to a Syrian village, then had the blindfold removed, you would probably think you were in our American Southwest viewing an Indian Pueblo, for here are the outdoor "beehive" ovens, the windmills, and waterwheels, the mesas and distant ant-Lebanon Mountains. East of Aleppo and Damascus, there is a desert to match the Sonora, vast and mystical. Some of the Middle Eastern craftwork, particularly the rugs, are similar in their design to Indian and Spanish designs. Historians believe that these parallels in culture and custom bespeak a common origin of people in West and East. One only needs to witness the Moors in Spain, whose descendants later brought their culture and their customs to the New World.

Every saga comes to an end, and so we said an emotional farewell to Aleppo and our wonderful host and hostess and boarded the fabled Taurus Express (a part of the Berlin to Bagdad system) to return to Istanbul. At the station we saw an unforgettable sight: a strikingly beautiful Syrian girl, saying farewell to a friend. It was not merely because of her grace and beauty that travelers turned to look, but she was unveiled and alone. Perhaps she was a Christian, or an extremely emancipated Muslim girl. The memory of that mysterious figure in black, standing in the Syrian sun, will remain with me always. Is it any wonder the Arab poets sing of Syria?

A sign showing the "Camel Way"
in Aleppo, Syria in 1933.

BOONDOGGLE OR BENEFIT

Perhaps few aspects of our Foreign Policy are more controversial than the U.S. Material Aids Program. Firsthand experience in the Middle East, however has shown that out there it is a "mixed bag" in its implementation. The percentage of its success, I believe, varies with the countries involved. A neutral business friend, who has lived in, and done business with, the Middle East for many years told a small group of us that he believed that a high percentage of the goals of aid had been realized in the Middle East. He estimated that seventy-five percent of the aid was delivered to the people, whereas some years ago European exporters of heavy machinery took it as a matter of course that they must send two machines if they expected to get one through intact.

The cliches one hears about our aid program are: "it seldom reaches the people whom it is meant to help," and "the funds or supplies rarely get beyond the rich and the powerful people who benefit at the expense of the poor." An angry, and frustrated journalist in an Arab city said one day, "When will your people (meaning Washington) learn the lesson that European countries have already learned, that it is far better to give aid in the form of persons who are experts from America, whom we can trust and respect, than to hand out money grants only?" The philosophy of "helping people help themselves" is a sound one in any nation.

The horror stories one hears about corruption, siphoning off supplies at the docks and airports, or selling American goods on the Black market are very often exaggerated. Some of the seeming corruption may be due to incompetence rather than greed. For example, in the freight years of Turkish Railways a few years ago one could see several rusted locomotives imported from the U.S.A. The truth was that the American and Turkish Engineers had miscalculated the height of the tunnels in Turkey, so all the smokestacks were too tall. They were duly disciplined, and the stacks adjusted.

I believe that it is safe to say that most of the persons handling deliveries in the Middle East were competent and honest. Our experience with the United Nations Refugee Works Agency and the Voluntary Agencies in bringing surplus foods (under Title IV), clothing and other supplies in for the refugees was a good one, partly because there was a tight security at dockside.

Many of us who were in the Middle East can speak firsthand of situations in Lebanon, Syria, Jordan, Gaza, Egypt and Israel, where UNRWA and the Voluntary Agencies handled tons of supplies to help feed and clothe refugees. Even during wartime or revolution, the American Aid reached people with remarkable regularity, and often at great risk to the volunteer workers. This good record was due largely to the integrity of people in UNRWA and the Voluntary Agencies, but also to a matching honesty and dedication to the needs of their people by nationals of the receiving countries. Supplies which disappeared were the exception.

A number of times when freighters arrived in the Port of Beirut with supplies for the refugees we were notified by Lebanese authorities that our representatives were welcome to go down into the holds of ships and check supplies themselves. On several occasions our colleague, Monsignor Ryan, the Co-Chairman of our Refugee Committee who represented Catholic Relief, joined us in visiting and checking the ships. We found very few irregularities. From stevedores and the clerks to the top Port officials, all were especially careful to see that containers marked "From Friends in America to Refugees in the Middle East" were delivered intact.

Aid to other than refugees was also delivered with a high rate of consistency and integrity. At one time Church World Service, the channel between American Churches and other voluntary agencies and the countries having need abroad, had the seventh highest volume of shipping from the United States. Within the aid program were many projects from road-building to airport construction from fruit-packing plants to administration of cities. Also there were administrative and engineering personnel sent out to work with the local people on a number of projects. (It is not my purpose to deal here with Military Aid, but I believe that their rate of delivery of goods and services was comparable with that of the Voluntary Agencies.)

One of the very important by-products of the Aid Program was the human contact between the American experts and the people in villages and towns where projects were located. Mr. C. A. Nichols, an elderly, retired Engineer from the Bell Telephone Company made many friends throughout the country even with a limited knowledge of Turkish. He advised local engineers in transforming an ancient French telephone system (installed in the time of the Sultans) to a modern dial system. In addition to his competence as an Engineer, Charles Nichols had also skill in human relations. All of those who worked with him remembered his patience and his smile. It had been the practice of the Turkish engineers in those early days to sit in their offices planning the overall strategy while the workmen worked on the lines. However, Charles did both office and line work and it started a new practice.

My friend from Robert College tells an amusing story of roadbuilding in the hinterland of Turkey where some American Engineers were surveying for a highway between a village and a county seat. The dialogue between the villagers and the Americans follows without editing:

THE MAYOR (speaking for the villagers): "Excuse me Engineer Efendi (sir) but our people would like to know what you are doing?"

THE ENGINEER: "Why we are getting ready to build a road with your Engineers."

(Silence and murmuring among the villagers.)

THE MAYOR: "But our people would like to know why you use so much string and poles and other equipment to build the road. Isn't that a lot of trouble?"

THE ENGINEER: (sipping a strong cup of Turkish coffee) "That is the way we build a road, Mr. Mayor. Please ask them how they build a road?"

(More murmuring among the villagers, more coffee and American cigarettes)

THE MAYOR: "The villagers say, Efendi, that when they build a road they just turn the donkey loose, and build the road where the donkey goes."

THE ENGINEER: "But, what if they don't have a donkey?"
(A long pause, and more whispering)
THE MAYOR: "Sir, they say if they don't have a donkey, then they
would call an American Engineer!"
(A sobering moment on both sides follows, then much laughter,
release of tension, and a warm invitation for the Americans to return
one day.)
THE MAYOR (smiling): "The villagers say that with your tools, and
'know-how', and with their wisdom and donkey, we shall build the
best road in Turkey, INSHALLAH (if God wills.)"

The author (background) with goat skin
water pail carrier in Silefkiye around 1932.

THE ANATOMY OF A REVOLUTION

In May, 1958, resentment and hostility among various political factions in Lebanon exploded almost overnight into a revolt which spread rapidly across the country. Some observers believe that the causes of the troubles were either a backlash from the violence which erupted in Iraq earlier in the spring or from the intrusion in Lebanese political affairs by the flamboyant President of the U.A.R. Abdul Gamal Nassar who had gained quite an emotional hold over most of the Arab nations in the Middle East. That is not to say that President Nassar did not also make some constructive contributions to Egypt and to Arab unity. Longtime observers of the situation felt that the troubles in Lebanon were mainly internal. One of these, a Professor at the American University in Beirut, found it ironic that President Eisenhower would dispatch a unit of the Sixth Fleet to the Eastern Mediterranean to support the Government of President Chamoun against an alleged Communist intrusion of the Lebanese Coast. The morning of the landing of troops from the Sixth Fleet several neighbors said, "We are in no more danger of an intrusion by the Communists than you are in America."

When one studies the History of Lebanon and her neighbors since the founding of the Republic of Lebanon in 1944, one realizes that the roots of the Revolution of 1958 were mainly within the country. From the time that Lebanon was separated from Mandated Syria (under the French) until the troubles in 1958, the people in Lebanon — Muslims, Christians and Jews — lived in relative harmony.

During these years the Lebanese political system which developed was, to say the least, peculiar and unique. According to a gentlemen's agreement, before every election the government would establish a balance of power based on a division of political leadership along sectarian lines. Hence the candidates were listed in the Press, and on the ballot, as follows:

- •The President (Maronite Christian)
- •The Prime Minister (Muslim)
- •The Foreign Secretary (Orthodox) (Greek Christian)

In the lower echelons of power there was an understanding that there would be Shiite and Sunnite Muslims, Druze (a Muslim sect in Syria and Lebanon), Maronites (Catholics, with their own patriarch and considerable independence from Rome), Protestants, Orthodox and Jews, all represented in the political structure. But this was a fragile balance at best; perhaps good in theory, but not so good in practice. With time power politics changed this system, until the non-Muslims held the balance of power even though the Christian and Muslim populations were almost equal in number. However, after the partition of Palestine, when the Arab Refugees were forced to flee their homeland, over 200,000 of them found refuge in Lebanon. With this influx of Palestinian refugees, most of whom were Muslim, a disbalance of Muslims over Christians caused concern to the Lebanese authorities so they decided to dispense with the census! This strategy, right or wrong, was blamed almost entirely on the Christian leaders. The disparity in power seems to have been one of the chief causes of the 1958 troubles. It was simply a question of the "outs" (Muslims) wanting to have more share in the leadership. In fact, at one time 17 of the 24 top posts in the Government were held by the Christians. (Note: The rebel forces were not Muslim only, but made up of a mix of sects, including some Christians, all of whom were seeking more power and say in the government. This struggle for power seemed to be the main cause of the troubles.)

However, as the status, education and competence of the Muslim population improved they wanted more opportunity and power. (Many of the Muslim youth as well as the Christian had been educated in the freer atmosphere of American, British and French schools. There was a saying that nearly half of the cabinets of leading Arab countries at one time had been trained in the American University in Beirut and the American University of Cairo in the Middle East.) It is important while considering the Middle East to remember that while most Turkish people are Muslims, they are not Arabs.

The close tie between sectarianism and politics in the Middle East has always been an enigma to the Westerner, accustomed to separation of Church and State. Many of the religious leaders are also deeply involved in politics, so it was not strange that they met together in a mountain retreat and agreed on a settlement which finally ended the 1958 revolution. One cannot go into detail here, but our diplomatic representatives, beginning with the Ambassador, were aware of the situation and played a sensitive and realistic role in helping with the final solution. One thing which helped was their approach to both sides.

Some of us who had watched the buildup of the troubles for several months were asked by embassy personnel for our personal opinion of the deploying of U.S. Marines in the Beirut area, and of the proposed landing and we advised against American interference in what was considered mainly an internal matter. While our advice was appreciated, we were told that the orders for the landing were set, and irreversible. We who were in nongovernmental work in Lebanon (i.e., religious missions, the colleges, the YMCA and the YWCA and other agencies) were most careful to remain nonpolitical, and this was respected by major parties.

Early one summer morning in 1958 units of the Sixth Fleet, U.S. Navy, which had been waiting off the Lebanese Coast moved out of the Mediterranean mist and from these ships American Marines came ashore in partial battle dress. Forward observers on the Navy craft were amazed to see Lebanese families swimming on the beach and curious crowds of people on shore watching. Fortunately, not a single gun was fired from either side. Moreover, there was a minimum of incidents between the Marines and the local forces. Any injuries or harm were also minimal for the duration. As he removed his warm gear, one Marine turned to his buddy and exclaimed, "Boy what a landing!" This is not to say that the ceasefire was permanent, for battles between the Rebel and Government forces continued. The U.S. forces standing at readiness were never seriously engaged in the local troubles.

During the week following the 1958 outbreak, representatives of the Voluntary Agencies in Lebanon met to discuss which relief measures were needed. This group chose a Catholic Monsignor, a Lebanese Protestant Pastor and myself (representing the YMCA and Church World Service) to serve as co-chairpersons of the Lebanon Emergency Committee. Muslim and

Christian Agencies of the country (Red Crescent Society, Muslim, Christian and Jewish leaders) were represented as consultants. It was interesting that the rebel and government forces were extremely careful not to harm any Jews. Also on the Committee were representatives of the YMCA, the United Nations Refugee Work Committee and Ex Officio represenation from the Embassy, serving as liaison in providing surplus foods for the victims.

The Lebanon Emergency Committee served throughout the troubles by providing food, clothing, medicines, and other assistance to over 30,000 refugees. The food was sent from the American people out of our surpluses. A representative of the International Red Cross stated that the LEC was the most ecumenical committee he had experienced. Both the government and rebel forces recognized the neutrality of the relief teams and allowed them to pass through the barbed-wire separating the government and rebel forces. The relief teams consisted of LEC committee members, Quakers, Mennonites and other voluntary agency personnel. One battle was delayed for two hours while a Danish rancher brought chickens from his farm in the mountains to feed the hungry! The Mennonite and Quaker workers who served in the Relief Centers were especially trusted by both sides. Joining them were Baptists who allowed our Committee to use their mission buildings located in rebel territory. The soup kitchens, established in both rebel and government areas, were a lifesaver, for during battles all local stores and markets were closed. David Karam, Chairman of the National Alliance of YMCA's, George Sleiman, Secretary of the Tripoli YMCA, and Ibrahim Chemayel, Secretary of the Beirut YMCA, all gave their leadership to the emergency. Miss Doris Boss, Advisor to the Lebanese YWCA's, did yeoman service with her colleagues. During all of the troubles David and Mona Karam remained in Tripoli and related to both sides with their advice and relief services. Mr. Karam's preparatory school, which served all of the youth of Northern Lebanon impartially, kept his school open throughout the troubles. Mr. and Mrs. Karam were lay persons in the YMCA and YWCA respectively. Finally, the international Committee of the YMCA in New York, and the World's Alliance of YMCA's in Geneva, gave both advice and staff assistance during and following the revolution. The relief work among the Palestinians in the refugee camps of Lebanon was particularly noteworthy.

As the revolution became more violent, foreigners were advised by their embassies to evacuate their families. While a number did so, others remained at their posts. A number of American business representatives and embassy staff stayed on. Dr. Harry Howard, First Secretary at our embassy, himself an authority on the Middle East, invited two of us, whose families were soon to be evacuated, to stay with him in his apartment on the edge of the city. Dr. Howard was of great assistance and support in the relief effort. The Lebanese leaders and people will not soon forget those who stuck it out. One Lebanese leader said, "We shall not forget how you remained, risking the danger with us; you were then no longer a foreigner, but a 'kardash' (brother)."

One evening while my family was still there with me, a blinding light passed through our kitchen, between our ten year old daughter and maid, followed by an explosion in the backyard. This was the 44th bomb to explode within a few blocks of our home. Arrangements were made for our family to be evacuated to the Swiss Alps, but my son and daughter wanted to stay with me. Three months later my family returned to Beirut. In the course of our voluntary work many of our committee risked their lives in serving both sides.

THE INCREDIBLE VOLUNTARY AGENCIES

In every thoughtful person's life there comes that moment when he, or she has to make a career choice. In my case it all happened almost casually while in Chicago Theological Seminary. One evening in 1929, it was announced the Dr. Cyril Haas, a medical missionary on leave from Turkey, would speak about his experiences in the Middle East. That evening I was torn between hearing the doctor or going to the opera. I chose the doctor and I believe it was one of the best choices of my life.

What Dr. Haas shared with us that evening in 1929 changed several lives. Strange how one sincere and committed man or woman can influence and change many others. In my naivete I stayed after the meeting and asked the doctor whether there would be a place for my training and talents in Turkey. Four months later I sailed on the Faber Liner, Providence, for the Mediterranean and Istanbul. There began a love affair with the Middle East, and twenty years of service with the American Board of the Congregational Christian Church and the YMCA in Turkey and the Arab countries.

Fortunately, on our ship there were several seasoned missionaries from the Middle East returning to their posts after furlough who took a very green young man in hand, taught him some Turkish and briefed him on the culture, religion and customs of lands still strange to him and to many Americans. Many times during the ensuing years I was grateful for that orientation which was far more relevant and real than the books about Turkey which I had been reading. To Cyril Haas, Miss Grace Towner and the others on the Providence, I owe so much for that education and inspiration, and their friendship during the years.

After a few days in fabulous Istanbul I took the Orient Express to Adana, in the South of Turkey, near Tarsus where I was to work on a boys' playground, and my new friends in Adana gave me far more. With a few words of Turkish and my tennis racket, and several butterflies in the pit of my stomach, I started to work.

The Turkish boys were my best teachers, although some of the vocabulary they taught me shocked a few ladies working at the American Lycee and the American Hospital, not to mention my Muslim teacher, Mehmet Ali Bey, who tried to overcome the street language with classical Arabic and Turkish. My very honest and helpful mentor, Miss Lillian Brauer, who had started the boys' playground some years before, understood my dilemma and reminded me that once you get past the "no-no" words, the best way to learn a language is through the young. She also reminded me that there are a few four-letter words which are among the finest in any language like love, work and many others. These I learned, and so could satisfy both the kids and the missionaries!

Many years before my arrival in Turkey the Presbyterian and Congregational Churches had wisely worked out a plan whereby the

Presbyterian mission would continue to work in the Arab countries and the Congregational mission in Turkey. This comity proved to be very appreciated by the nationals of the countries, and accepted by their governments, for it was a solution to those who had been confused by the many approaches of different denominations. One of the Muslim teachers on the playground said something very true, "You have one Allah just as we have, but you certainly have a lot of different churches!"

Under the new Turkish Republic, established in 1924, a government decree forbad the teaching of religion to persons under 18 years of age. This decree included religious teaching of minors by the Muslim Mullahs as well as Christian and other teachers of various sects. As a secular state anxious to throw off the former limiting aspects of the Muslim and other religions, Turkey continued this policy until such time as the government was convinced that there would be a true separation of church and state. Foreign missionaries and teachers respected the law and were trusted. Aside from this aspect of religious education among the youth there were no serious curbs on religious worship, practices or programs. The law merely restricted the formal teaching of religion among minors without affecting the services to persons of all ages in clinics, schools and colleges, hospitals and other institutions.

During the hot summers in Adana (with temperatures at times 120° in the shade, and precious little shade) we worked in the Taurus Mountains 60 miles away near a Turkish village. There, the American teachers, doctors, social workers and nurses had their holidays and conducted a Summer Camp for underprivileged children. It was in the mountains one day that I experienced my "baptism of fire" when the villagers came to protest our use of what they called "their water from Allah." Alone at the camp that day I decided to use my few words of their language to calm their anger and let them know that the water supply was ample for the village and for the camp. With my first feeble attempt to put it all into Turkish, they became less angry and stopped digging up our waterpipes. The dialogue went something like this (their part was in down-to-earth Turkish, which I could understand; mine was very limited and rather childish):

THEY: "Gench Efendi" (young man). "This is our water from Allah. You have no right to it."

EY: "Alfedersiniz" (forgive me). "But your Muhtar (Mayor of Birijik) said we could use it."

THEY: "Allah af et, Muhtar" (may God forgive the Mayor). "What does he care about our needs?"

A pause; some giggling from the women of the village in the background, which gave me fresh courage. Freely translated these were my words:

EY: "You man, I man. Why we fight? 'Allah' is One; we must be one; forgive my poor Turkish, please. I new in your beautiful village; why we not friends?"

(The Muhtar began to laugh, and all then joined in; I with them; then we all had coffee and they said "Say more Turkish; it sounds just like Laurel & Hardy on our movie soundtrack.")

From then on there was no more demonstration, or anger, and whenever I went through the village they would give me a warm "Mr. Yank," for they could not pronounce the soft "g" in their language. After that encounter I remember what the Prophet Mohammed said one day to his followers: "Learn another language than your own, for each language is a person." Certainly I had lost no time in adding to my language skill.

That knowledge of Turkish helped us return to the Middle East again during the Second World War when the YMCA, looking for a World Service Secretary to serve as Advisor to the "Amerikan Dershane" recruited me. It is interesting that one can no more forget a language one has learned than how to drive a car or swim. After a gap of eight years since leaving Turkey, the language came back in a few weeks.

In the chapter on Kemal Ataturk, Emancipator of Turkey, we spoke of the earlier days in Turkey and how our voluntary agencies had a vital role in helping the people of the Republic to train and equip themselves in building their new nation. For over 175 years there has been an American presence in Turkey which has weathered political unrest, changes in Government, wars and earthquakes and vast reforms. In all of this time, even when Turkey and America did not always agree as nations, our representatives have, for the most part, been liked and respected. In the case of the missionaries they have been loved. Serving in schools, colleges, hospitals, publications, social work and general missionary work as well as YMCA's and YWCA's and church outreach for Protestant nationals, their emphasis has been to "help the people help themselves," and to train nationals to take over the work. In one of the briefings by the International Committee of the YMCA before going back to Turkey I was told, "You will help to train others to take over your job." After twelve years as a fraternal worker in the YMCA in Turkey, I did just that. As witness to the popularity of and affection for the schools and the YMCA and YWCA, there has always been a waiting list for entrance to them, even in wartime and revolution. They have only been closed when crossfire or total destruction prevented people from being in the streets.

In Cairo a story is still told about the riots in that city, when the mobs roamed the streets, stoning and destroying foreign buildings in their rage (during the former regime in Egypt) at the powers which had exploited them. Not a single mission building, the Y's or the American University were harmed. In fact, when a group began to climb the fence in front of the YMCA a young man in the grounds yelled, "Don't destroy that place, for it is ours; it belongs to us, and it helps us." The mob withdrew. In the Scutari Mission School (Lycee) for Turkish young women, an Armenian teacher was asked why the Turkish girls loved her so much when the Turks and Armenians had, in the past, been enemies. She said, "I guess they love me for I love them."

With the years, more and more Americans came to the Middle East as diplomats, teachers and advisors to industry, agriculture, education and in countless fields. One of them said to a group of Missionaries, "We could not have come had it not been for your influence and service here all these years." Our answer was, "That was only a part of it, for the people of these lands have a quality, and a deep desire to learn, which created a climate where we were welcome."

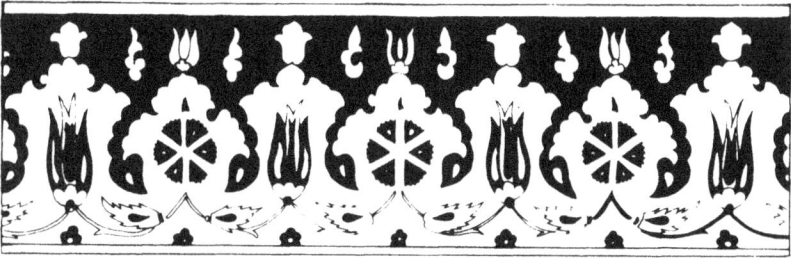

WELCOME SIXTH FLEET

The Battleship Missouri, on whose deck the Japanese representatives signed the surrender after World War II, was the first U.S. Navy vessel to visit Turkey after V-Day in Europe. It brought the body of Ambassador Ertegun back to Turkey after his death in Washington. The Ambassador was Dean of the Diplomatic Corps and was loved and respected in America. When I was invited to serve in Turkey by the International YMCA, Senator Alben Barkely arranged an interview in Washington for me with Ambassador Ertegun in 1942. I shall never forget the kindness of the Erteguns at the Embassy in Washington, nor Ambassador Ertegun's advice and help with letters to friends in Turkey. Surely he made the way smoother for my second assignment in Turkey.

The city of Istanbul made all efforts to give warm welcome to the Missouri, partly because the Navy had honored Turkey by returning their beloved Ertegun to his homeland, and partly because 1946, the year of the visit, was a high point in Turkey's friendship with the Americans. The night before the fleet arrived, one could feel the excitement of the people and one could read, spread between the minarets of the Blue Mosque, an enormous sign, saying, "WELCOME MISERY," No offense was meant in the spelling; it was just that "ouri" in "Missouri" did not make a sound familiar to the Turkish people. When the visit ended, the morning paper carried a front-page cartoon, showing the SS Missouri loaded down with hearts.

Early on the next morning of the SS Misouri's arrival every available boat, taxi, private car, street car and bus was crowded bringing the people down to Dolmabache, the landing-place, to see the largest naval vessel most had ever seen. Miss Phoebe Clary, Advisor to the Girls' Dershane (YWCA) and Co-Chairman of the USO Committee, and I went out to the Missouri with the Naval Attache to discuss the Canteen and shore program planned by the USO Committee with the aid of Turkish representatives. It was a thrill, but only the first of some 44 visits of the Sixth Fleet by other vessels. Our job at the YMCA was to plan sports and sightseeing events. My wife served with the Canteen, along with many American women and their Turkish counterparts. In fact, the Turkish women found a number of families where parents allowed their daughters to come to the Canteen to serve as hostesses. Miss Clary and her staff at the YWCA had a great deal to do with the delicate planning of the hostess program. Some of the best known families in Istanbul supported the Canteen, and permitted their daughters to attend. So far as we know there was not a single serious incident during the 44 visits of the Sixth Fleet. This, no doubt, was due to the careful planning, and to the fine behavior of most of the sailors and officers. No small credit is due to Turkish friends who trusted the Y's, and who were anxious to show that in spite of their past history of discrimination against women, they now had a much more liberal point of view. An Admiral with the fleet expressed deep appreciation to the USO

Committee and to Phoebe Clary and myself, not only for the planning but for our briefings on the customs and traditions of the Turks when we went aboard. As the British would say, "good show."

There was, however, one incident at a dance in the Mens' Dershane Gymnasium that was blown out of all proportion by the extremist press in Istanbul. At a perfectly chaperoned and decorous party a photographer slipped in and took pictures of dancers, well-behaved in fact but distorted in making the prints, so that it seemed they were misbehaving. Again, Turkish and American chaperones were conducting a very wholesome and friendly party which one observer called "no more harmful than a Sunday School picnic." When the din over this incident subsided, more members than ever came to the Dershane, and we were thoroughly exonerated by the Admiral of the Fleet Unit, as well as by the Turkish authorities.

One of the delightful events organized by the USO and by the Girls' Dershane, was a boarding party for younger boys and girls who were either underprivileged or handicapped. Other children from the Turkish and American communities were included in some of these visits to the Fleet. Our daughter, Maja, who was then about five years old, thoroughly enjoyed these occasions and believes that one reason why she is in the US Navy today is because of this experience with the Sixth Fleet. But most delightful of all was the way in which the sailors enjoyed these visits as they guided the children around the ships. Perhaps this did as much for Turkish-American friendship as any other event.

During Fleet visits, the Navy cooperated in furnishing food and Navy Personnel to aid the Canteen. They also gave assistance, equipment and support to the shore program of sports and sightseeing. In particular, the Physical Education Department of the Ministry of Education loaned us two capable leaders who met with us in pre-planning sessions so that all sports events and sightseeing went smoothly. But the most rewarding results came through basketball, swimming (Istanbul's waters are an ideal place for all aquatic events and Mr. Suat Erler, a former Olympic swimming champion, was tireless and of the greatest help to the water phase of shore activities), softball, tennis, wild boar hunting and greased wrestling (ancient sport of the Turks). To the astonishment of the Navy personnel, they found they they were no match for the Turkish wrestlers and that there were Turkish basketball teams of amateur status who could beat the Navy.

In one basketball game a Junior Officer in charge of welfare expressed his admiration for the sportsmanship and skill of the Turkish team. When we told him that there were only about 15 basketballs in all of Turkey, he said, "Why we have 20 in this Fleet Unit alone." Happily, at the half the Admiral presented the Turkish Captain with two new basketballs.

Other incidents during the visits, some amusing, some sad and some heart-warming, are worth recording. One incident involved a small newsboy who was selling the Evening Edition to pasersby. He was overcome when some sailors bought all of his papers, then re-sold them to the public, giving the money to the newsboy.

"Hamals" (porters with large baskets who carry incredible loads through the streets) often lined up in front of bars where sailors sometimes drank a bit too much "oozu" (or raki, a colorless liquor made from pressed grape seeds which turns white when water is added) so they could carry the sailors back in their baskets in safety, if not comfort, to their ships. They really were concerned for their safety, for like every large city, Istanbul had its "street people" who would exploit such a situation.

In another incident, a very polite but lonely sailor said to me, "Mr. Young, a reporter from a Turkish newspaper asked me what I think of his city, and especially the traffic. What should I tell him?" I advised the truth. The next morning the headlines stared at us, "American sailor states Istanbul traffic is weird and wild and we agree! The American asked the reporter why our taxi drivers use their horns instead of their brakes and steering-wheels."

Once some sailors found some boys kicking a string ball around in a poor neighborhood. They joined them in play and were amazed at their dexterity, especially in using their heads (soccer is a national sport along with greased wrestling) to knock the ball just where they wanted. The next day the sailors returned to the field and gave two new soccer balls to the kids.

Our daughter, Maja, and son, David, were of great help to us in time of Fleet visits. Sometimes we would have several basketball games going simultaneously in different parts of the city. All the time our daughter teased her brother about how she would see the Admiral, and she did the night he presented basketballs to the Turkish team.

Home visits were special during this time. This is where the American ladies organized special events in homes. I can still see a dozen sailors in one of our homes sitting on Turkish cushions on the floor, munching potato chips and leafing over old magazines. These parties usually included a swim, sightseeing in mosques and castles, and just a good talk with "the girl next door."

When one of the carriers came in, basketball was played on the deck and everybody had such a great time that nothing would do but that the Navy show a game of American football. A Turkish Engineer who had graduated from the University of Minnesota explained the game to the crowd in one of the largest stadiums but failed to prepare the Turkish spectators with "why the stretchers." Just before the game the stretchers were carried to the edge of the field and wild applause broke from the great crowd. Later, the Turks explained that if this were their game, the stretchers would be used for injured referees, and not players. As a matter of fact, an American quaterback was injured in the game and was carried off the field. Then there was a sad sigh from the crowd!

At a final ball, given in the Dolmabache Palace on the Bosphorous, the Admiral and the Governor of the Province exchanged toasts and compliments, and both remarked about the wonderful friendliness and lift the week had brought to Turkey and the Navy. That was "the week that was" so much in so many ways.

THE DELI KANLIS ('CRAZY BLOODS') YOUTH

The term used to designate "youth" among the people of Turkey is deli kanli or "crazy bloods." This rather colorful term might be applied in all nations of the Middle East and, in fact, to youth in all of the nations of the world. Certainly in dealing with young people of the Middle East for two decades I was often aware that they had a built-in anger and passion which could erupt on provocation. When this passionate anger was held in check, they were magnificent, idealistic and very likeable; when they were angry, and sometimes irresponsible for their actions, one often could not blame them, but the world they lived in.

We know that some unprincipled leaders often exploited the youth's idealism and whipped up their anger for their (the leaders) own political ends. In the past 75 years, time and again, the youth have been roused and thrust forward on the growing edge of revolt. In today's news reports on television how many times we see youth out of control leading the mobs in cities like Teheran. More constructive leaders have not used youth in this manner. In Egypt, during former regimes there was a saying "He who controls the youth controls the 'street' (the political situation)."

There are ways to damp down the "crazy bloods" without repressing them; there are options to violence which they are apt to respond to if the options are presented in a positive way by someone whom they respect and admire. Early in 1924 Turkish Revolution there were some hotheads who decided to march on the Sultan's Palace and to destroy the Sultan. Kemal Ataturk, leader of the revolution, acted promptly before things got out of hand persuading the rioters that it would serve the New Turkey far better to ignore the Sultan and let him go free. Someone once said, "A good leader always has alternatives in crisis; this is why he is a leader."

During the recent (1970's) revolution in Lebanon, the YMCA's in that country conceived a plan for "turning the street-fighters around," and training them for reconstruction of their city rather than destruction of it. With most of these young men it worked; their passion and anger came under control when they had leaders whom they could count on for direction.

Ghassan Sayyah, General Secretary of the Lebanese YMCA headed up this unusual project. He could not have had a better advisor than Mr. Harry Brunger, veteran overseas secretary, and my able successor in Beirut, now on the headquarters staff of the international division of the YMCA in New York City.

Often an alternative to anger is logic. In my memory is a young man who grew very angry with us at the "Dershane" in Istanbul because we would not agree to teach him enough English in four weeks to be eligible for a student visa to the United States. He said, "Well, you can have your English course, for I am going to another organization where they promise a three week's course to learn English." Our answer was, "By all means do so, but remember, the Consulate will not grant a visa unless you know enough of the language to succeed in college." He was adamant and very angered, stomping out of the office. We decided if he came back we would not make an issue of his response. The next day a very sheepish young man waited in the office of our "Yar Director" (Assistant Director) to see me. Esat Kural, who had a special gift for keeping cool and objective said, "I believe this young man has shown a lot of courage; now he wants to talk with us." "Here I am, Mr. Young, I am sorry for my behavior yesterday, because you would not do what I wished, but you and Mr. Kural were very honest and sincere with me while all they were interested in at the other school was my fee. I have decided to take your three month's course, if you will accept me." He was bright, determined and no longer angry. In two months he had learned enough to secure his visa. While at his university in America he won a fellowship for graduate studies in "Trusteeship Administration" and still works for the United Nations. When he invited us to dinner in New York we remembered that frustrating day at the "Y" and were able to smile about it.

The energy and idealism of our youth, when rightly channeled, can be a constructive force in a nation and in the world. In a study made a few years ago college students were asked to name the persons they most admired. When it came to the political field most of them could not name a single political leader whom they could completely trust and follow.

Who knows, there may be a potential leader of character and courage in some small nation who will lead us out of "our crisis in character." After all, in Roman times there was a young carpenter from Nazareth who was thought by many even in his own town as unlikely to become a leader of men.

Some years ago at a banquet honoring a YMCA Secretary, tribute was paid to him because he stayed in a small job, in a small town in spite of offers of far more lucrative and important jobs in large cities. He was a Boys' Work Secretary. As he responded to the good things said about him he said, "The honors you have given me tonight I shall always treasure, but the greatest honor I have had is to have known two generations of youths by their first names." This is the kind of leadership the world is waiting for.

In memory I think of another potential leader from the other side of the world, Nicholas Goncharoff, a Soviet tank Commander in World War II, a prisoner of war in Germany, from where he finally escaped to the American Lines. He relates how, while in prison, a YMCA Secretary from neutral Sweden visited him bringing reading matter and encouragement. Nicholas said that the other visitors talked to him only about their sect and what it would do for him, but that the "Y" man brought a deck of cards and played a game with him. In the midst of the hopelessness and cynicism of prison he had found a friend. Later Nicholas studied in Munich; after graudation he was invited to America by the YMCA where he found all he had been searching for. "Whenever," he said, "I see that sign YMCA, I think of the words, 'You made Christianity attractive.'"

As I left the Middle East in the early sixties, the Egyptian YMCA invited me to be their guest in Alexandria where they gave me a surprise dinner in my honor. Our dear friend, John Kirmiz, Secretary of the Alexandria YMCA, organized the event. Instead of a small group of friends, there were all of the students I had known in a training center high in the lovely Lebanese mountains where I served as dean for two years. On that occasion so moving for me they presented a copper medallion to me, "To E. Porter Young, in apprecia-

tion for his valuable services to youth through the YMCA's in Arab countries."
It meant more to me than any citation or degree I have ever had. It will always
be a memory to me of the Hasans, Mehmets, Mustafas, Hamits, the Arams
and Constantines and Toledos, and all of the other youth who came into my
life and enriched and inspired me to be better than I am for their sake.

The 1933 volley ball team
in Adana, Turkey in the American playground.

INCIDENT ON THE BULGARIAN BORDER

In 1960 the Young family — my wife, son, daughter and myself — took a long journey by car from Beirut, Lebanon to Europe. The adventure was unique in three respects: the main purpose for our trip was to take our two adopted children back to visit their homeland in Bavaria; second, 1960 was the only time in recent years when there was no unrest or revolution in any of the countries we passed through, and third, it was the first time after World War II that Bulgaria opened its doors to the West.

You can imagine the mounting excitement as we left Beirut and traversed Lebanon, Syria, Turkey, Bulgaria, Yugoslavia, Austria, Germany, Switzerland, Lichtenstein and Italy, returning to Beirut by steamer from Genoa. Our son, David, parted from us in Genoa to take ship for America to begin his college career.

Of course Turkey, where we had spent a number of years was like "old home week." We had left that country in 1953 and it was good to be back now seven years later. For the week we were in Istanbul, that beautiful city on the Bosphorous, our friends gave us little time for rest. Turkey had changed a great deal, but it was a happy "homecoming" for the most part even though some of our dearest friends were no longer living.

In Istanbul we met old friends from the Adana days, and my former colleagues at the Dershane (YMCA), Esat Kural and Homer Kalchas and their wives entertained us and helped us in every way to find friends and to proceed on our way to Europe. Esat had been our faithful friend and competent associate in the Dershane, and Homer, devoted friend of many years had been head of our Language School and a Boys' Worker. Esat Bey's wife, Suat, a very lovely and modern Turkish woman, was a credit to her country. Evelyn Lyle Kalchas, originally an Australian Journalist, met Homer through the YMCA while looking for a guide to show her the city! Evelyn, now a Turkish citizen wrote several books about Turkey. In fact, she is accepted and liked in Turkey and her talents were appreciated. Both Esat and Homer came to the USA under YMCA auspices for a year of in-service training in the YMCA and they each had a great deal to do with the growth, and services of the Amerikan Dershane.

With some misgivings about our success in securing a Bulgarian Transit visa, Esat Bey and I visited the Bulgarian Consulate in Istanbul and were met with surprising cordiality. Two days later we were rolling through European Turkey (Thrace) enroute to the Bulgarian border. The last time I had been there was as an interpreter for a Church World Service Mission to meet Russian refugees who had been held in Bulgaria during the war and that was a dangerous trip. I could not help but wonder whether my name might be on some black list in one of the files in "that little room" next to every frontier customs post. Happily, we sailed through without the slightest trouble. In fact our automobile was among the first American motor cars to travel through

Bulgaria.

At the Turkish checkpoint the Turkish officials were kindness itself. It so happened that the man in charge turned out to be a former student at the Dershane. Nothing we could say would dissuade him from inviting us to lunch. He was a charming host, regaling us with stories of what had happened on the border during the war. He was particularly attentive to Maja, our daughter, and Dave, our son. Also, he introduced us to his opposite number on the Bulgarian side. In Turkish customs there was a minimum of inspection of car and baggage and then we crossed into Bulgaria. All of our anxieties about Bulgaria were set to rest. They tried to outdo the Turks in hospitality so we not only had coffee but another luncheon.

The only excitement at the Bulgarian checkpoint was caused by a British motorist who was very upset and angry because the border official found one signature missing on his motor transit permit. (Why is it when we have to deal with foreign officials and find no common language, we think that if we just shout loud enough in English we will be understood?)

Since the Bulgarian customs man knew Turkish, I offered to be interpreter, but only on condition that my British acquaintance would calm down. After coffee for us, and tea for the British guest, we all felt more relaxed and the permit was granted. However, we had noticed a mysterious man on a motorcycle at the barrier looking very bored and we were informed that we must take the main road through Sofia and be accompanied by the motorcyclist.

In Turkish the Bulgarian Guard, now friendly with us, whispered to us, "Mr. Yank Efendi, you and your family can go alone without the motorcycle, for we trust you," whereupon the British gentleman became furious with me. I can still see him standing in the middle of the road waving his arms at me. That ended the incident at the Bulgarian border, but it did not end the trip through Bulgaria. As we closed that chapter and drove toward Sofia through the beautiful hills and farmland, we wondered what excitement would be ahead.

Before we left Istanbul, a Socony freind presented us with two quarts of motor oil and a quart of transmission fluid. Little did we realize that this gift was like gold. Of course, we had been told that the gas in Bulgaria was very low octane. Halfway between Svilingrad and Sofia we stopped in the one gas station in a provincial town where the attendant greeted us like a brother, informing us, "I have a brother in Chicago. Do you know him?" We admitted that we had been in Chicago for a while, but that it was bigger than Sofia so we had not met his brother. "Let me show you the gift my brother brought me," he said. With furtive looks over his shoulder he took us to a backroom where he unveiled his brother's gift, a Ford compact. Said he sadly, "I have not been able to drive it for some time because it needs oil not available here. I saw a can of oil in the back of your car. Please give me that, and I will fill your tank with gasoline." We gave him the quart of that precious liquid. But we paid for our gas.

In Sofia all tourists stay in the official hotel. Upon arriving, the children and I walked out to see the town. We were hungry for fresh fruit after the long, dusty trip and we found a fruit stand with a long line of people waiting to be served. (The hotel had thoughtfully furnished us with ration cards, but we wanted the experience of standing in line!) From there we found a discotheque and snackbar and a stout attendant said he knew English, "I have brother in Chicago," he confided in a low voice. My son observed, "Dad, does everyone in Bulgaria have a brother in Chicago?" It was not long before a crowd of young people invited our kids into a booth, and I had the wisdom to stay where I was and let them talk. When they came back Maja said, "They offered Dave five dollars for his jeans, but is he dumb. He refused."

We all agreed that the visit in Bulgaria was a good experience.

A camp water carrier deep in the Taurus mountains
near Tarsus in 1932.

NUMBER TWENTY-THREE
ALEMDAR CADDESI AVENUE

Like Rome, one might say that Istanbul is "a city set on seven hills" and at the top of one of those hills between the Sultan's Saray (Palace), now a museum, and the ancient Church of Aya Sophia (Sanctia Sophia) is the Mens' Dershane (former YMCA) where it was my privilege to spend eleven years in service as Advisor and Acting Director of a school and social center for men and boys. Here in the "Old City" were a gymnasium, a dormitory for university students, a restaurant, a playground, a gameroom (with billiards, table games, a library and adjoining meeting-rooms) and staff offices. At the heart of this operation were the gym program for all ages and a school of languages and commerce. Outside the city on the beautiful Sea of Marmara was a new summer camp which always had a waiting list.

One of the first things I learned was that basketball, summer camping and group work had been introduced to Turkey by the YMCA and YWCA, predecessors of the two Dershane (one for boys and the other for girls.) The girls' Dershane was a few blocks away, also in the Old City. The cooperation between the two organizations was most helpful. While there may have been pressure for both of these American/Turkish centers to be established in the modern part of the city (Pera), the founders believed that a move to the Old City would identify them more closely with the Muslim majority in Istanbul.

Having come out to the Middle East in 1942 on a freighter which took sixty days for the voyage around Africa because of the Second World War, my wife was not able to join me until two years later. So along with some other American "war widowers," I lived at Kennedy Lodge on the campus of Robert College overlooking the Bosphorous. Our host was Dr. Livvy Wright, the new President of Robert College and an authority on Turkey and the Middle East as well as a former professor at Princeton. One could not have had a finer introduction to Turkey than through Dr. Wright, Robert College and the staff at the Mens' Dershane and seasoned Dershane Board members of many nationalities.

Ilhami Polater Bey, who had been Physical Director of the Dershane, had acted as director of the organization during the interim between two American advisors. He was a valued friend and mentor, also one of the pioneers in camping in the earlier YMCA. Ilhami Bey also was invited to have in-service training in the YMCA's of the United States.

In pioneering the YMCA's abroad, they were encouraged to become self-directing, self-supporting and indigenous. Whatever funds were granted were always predicated on financial support in the host country. Usually, the Fraternal Secretaries (or World Service Secretaries) salaries and expenses for travel, etc., were provided by funds from the North American YMCA's (the USA and Canada). More and more of the support of the overseas YMCA's came from the host countries so they felt that the YMCA, or Dershane in

Turkey, were their organizations. At the same time the Boards of Directors of the Y's were increasingly composed of people of the country. Hence our Board was made up of Muslims, Christians and Jews. Col. Cuthbert Binns, a British business man in Istanbul, and Prof. Laurens Seelye, Professor at the American Girls' College at Arnavutkoy (a suburb of Istanbul), were two very distinguished Dershane Chairmen.

At the same time the wives of board members formed a Ladies Auxiliary to the Dershane, which helped greatly in the development of the center. On this Auxiliary were prominent Turkish women who gave their valuable time to the Dershane program. A panel of honorary advisors, consisting of distinguished Turkish and foreign leaders were invited to Board Meetings, but were ex officio. Finally, and not least, a number of American Board (Congregational) missionaries, who had been instrumental in starting the YMCA in Turkey, continued to give their valuable services on the Board. Dr. Fred Field Goodsell was a founder of the YMCA in Turkey. Many of the Honorary Advisors: lawyers, business men, educators, oil executives and government officials gave their time to advise and help the Dershane.

During the transition years from the Dershane period to a completely indigenous organization, Esat Kural, our Yar Direktor, gave yeoman service, as did interim American advisors and Homer Kalchas, head of the language school. Among all of the staff from the International Committee in New York City and from the World Alliance of YMCA's in Geneva, Dr. Paul Anderson and Dr. Paul Limbert gave of their wisdom and rich experience.

Through the years, the former YMCA and its successor, the Dershane, grew in membership and influence. At one time a leading educator in the Ministry of Education called the Dershane "the finest evening school in Turkey." The Turkish "Kizilay" (Red Crescent Society) requested Ilhami Polater and myself to give part-time in advising its youth division in the development of a summer camp program. During World War II we travelled freely throughout most of Turkey experiencing warm welcome and cooperation wherever we went. The Red Crescent Society asked us to prepare, in Turkish a guide book for camp leaders and also cooperated with us in forming centers for youth leadership training. Again, Ilhami Bey, and our fine physical director, Sabri Besen Bey, played important roles in both of these developments. The Director of the Red Crescent Society, Dr. Ramzi Gonench, was most supportive.

Perhaps most vital of all were the educational, social and character-training programs within the institution itself. One Turkish citizen of Greek background said to our Turkish director one day, "Here I learned to know and like persons of other races and nationalities as I had never done before. At our Dershane we parked our differences at the door to be brothers."

In all of our YMCAs in the Middle East the relationship with other youth organizations, indigenous to the countries involved, became a warm and friendly one once both sides realized that they had much to give each other.

And then there was not only brotherhood in the Dershane but occasional humor. I was spared the rather embarrassing experience of one of my predecessors who on arrival in Istanbul was given a welcome by students, faculty and staff. One of the most popular workers in our building was Hamit Efendi, the head janitor, who insisted on being called Bey. Hamit was a very proud man. But because his knowledge of English was limited, he asked some of the Turkish University students in the dormitory to brief him in what to say to the newcomer. This was a temptation too strong for the students to resist. As the American passed down the reception line he came to Hamit, who bowed very low, and said with great dignity (prompted by the students, of course), "How are you, sir, you old son of a gun?" With great aplomb and a ready wit, the American replied, "Thank you Hamit Bey. I have heard about your good work and I hope you and I will be friends." The new director certainly won that round!

Edirne Kafi (Adrianople Gate) or Western Gate,
in an ancient burial ground in Istanbul in 1932.

PARDON MY TURKISH

When our ship landed in Istanbul in the Spring of 1930 I knew three words and one phrase in Turkish. The words were "Marhaba" (hello), "Nasilsiniz?" (how are you?) and "Inshallah" (if God wills); the phrase was "Gechmish olsun" (may it pass). Soon I discovered that the words were all right, but that the phrase "Gechmish olsun" was limited to offering comfort to the ill. It meant literally, "may you be better soon." However, a few days later when I made my first venture alone on a very crowded tram rather than push my way through at destination, I said in a loud voice, "Gechmish olsun," meaning for me, "Please move so I can pass." This was met with no response, only stolid stares, until a kindly young man intervened and a way was made for me. Very politely he said in English, "I think you had better learn some more Turkish before you go out alone again. I am a graduate of Robert College so let me know if I can help you." As I left the tram I realized that "thank you" was still not in my vocabulary so I said the next best thing, "Nasilsiniz?" All seemed to relax, smiled and all began to talk Turkish at once. To my new friend I said, "What are they saying?" "He will learn, Inshallah, if God wills," he replied. At that moment I felt a warmth toward these people that seldom failed me during many years in Turkey. It was my baptism into a new land and a new language.

When we left Turkey the last time, I was the possessor of a respectable vocabulary of some 4,000 words, a good stock of parables, and still some modesty about my knowledge. On almost the last day before sailing with my family to America in 1953 we went to a favorite restaurant with friends for a farewell meal. They had just praised my Turkish when I ordered figs in syrup for dessert. The waiter, an old friend, would not correct me in front of others but took me to one side and said, "Mr. Yank, do you know what you ordered? It was the New Testament in syrup." I had forgotten that "incir" (fig) and "incil" (New Testament) can easily be confused. Perhaps this experience was meant to prevent any false pride I might have had in knowledge of the language.

Turkish, with its newly written alphabet and its phonetical sounds, would seem to be an easy language to learn. Unfortunately, it is anything but easy. For one thing, to really learn Turkish one needs to know some Persian and Arabic words, as well as the pure, but limited dialect which the Turks brought with them when they migrated from Asia.

It is said that Turkish, or dialects resembling Turkish, are spoken from Hungary to China. During the reign of Sultan Suleiman the Magnificent, almost all of the Mediterranean ports came under control of the Turkish Imperial Navy commanded by Admiral Barbarosa, another giant of Ottoman times. Therefore, historians report that one could hear Turkish all the way from Istanbul to Venice. Moreover, elderly Arabs in nations South of Turkey who had been functionairs during the Ottoman occupation of the Levant, spoke Turkish fluently, and still do so in the privacy of their homes.

Classical Turkish contains many words derived from Arabic. Arabic was also the language of the Muslim Holy men and many of the religious writings were originally written in the Arabic script. In Turkey the Koran was first translated from the Arabic alphabet into the new Turkish alphabet under the reforms of Ataturk. However, in more recent years, even in Turkey, the scholars have turned to the ancient writings and the Government has relaxed its rules regarding the use of the Arabic script. This leniency is to be commended because the richness and depth of the Arabic language, as well as the imagery and poetry of Persian, have enriched the Turkish culture and thought.

The phonetic character of the modern Turkish language has enabled the Turks to Westernize their language and thus help communication and trade with the West. An example of this adaptation is their taking certain words from English and adding a vowel to the front of them (the Turks do not begin any words with a consonant.) Hence in a book, magazine or newspaper one is startled to see such words as "Istatistik," "Ispor" (sport) and "Istanbul," or to hear them in the spoken language. Sometimes this phoneticism leads to extremes, as when one sees on a menu otherwise written in proper Turkish, the item "Ayrish tu" (which means Irish stew, since the "ay" is pronounced like "I" in our language.)

However, some of the most charming phrases are written by students learning English, like one over-eager young man, who ended a letter to his teacher with "And do give my affectionate sensations to your high-lived companion," or another who wrote, also to his teacher, "At the American Hospital, the doctor graciously took my stomach out with some salts, and I feel better." No doubt some of our Turkish is just as bizarre for them.

American missionaries in summer retreat in 1933.
(Author is at right on back row.)

THE CHILDREN'S HOURS

The Summer of 1950 proved to be one of the memorable periods in our life together, for it was the year of the Oberammergau Passion Play and the year in which we adopted two German children. Our Staff at the Dershane in Istanbul decided that it was time for us to have a holiday, so we chose to visit Bavaria and the Passion Play. Little did we know as we sailed toward Venice on a summer day that on return from Germany we would be a family of four.

While in the Bavarian Alps that summer we met and became friends with a German woman doctor. When we told her how eager we were to adopt a child, she put us in touch with Frau Stautner, director of the youth division of the post-war government in Munich who had as one assignment the placing of German war orphans in American homes. Ours were the first adoptions involving foreign civilians; up to that time all of the arrangments had been made for military personnel who wished to adopt children. As the steps toward adoption were taking place, Frau Stautner asked whether we would like to make arrangements through the Allied Occupation in Germany, or directly with the new German government. We decided upon the latter, and they were so pleased that we did so that the whole process was speeded up. Many of the arrangements were made within two weeks.

I then had to return to my responsibilities in Turkey, so I left my wife to complete the process and to fly back to Istanbul with the children. (Originally we had planned the adoption of only one child, but when my wife cabled that she had found a boy and a girl we were delighted.) Maja and David have been such a blessing and a joy to us that we no longer think of them as adopted.

Certainly, as I went out to the airport on the night they arrived the excitement was almost too much. While waiting for the plane to arrive from Munich, a Turkish friend invited me for coffee. When I told him that Mrs. Young was returning from Germany with two children, he was speechless and could only say "Mashallah" (what wonders God hath wrought). Then I understood that he thought it a miracle that a middle-aged couple could produce two children on a summer holiday. I then explained it all to him. He looked relieved.

My first glimpse of our new family was through the gate next to customs. First came a little girl bouncing a ball in a string bag followed by her adopted brother, very concerned over the attention given his sister by the curious crowd. Then came my wife, almost unrecognizable under layers of coats and lighter baggage, and I champing at the bit because it was the only time I had not found friends to help me get out to the plane! The children's shyness and strangeness wore off when we got to our Jeep, waiting patiently to take us through the old city to their new home. That Jeep, later christened by some Turkish boys as "the infidel's donkey," was a delight to both children and before we got home through the winding streets of Istanbul, David was already telling me in German that he wanted to learn to drive, too. The children knew only a smattering of English, but that did not matter; there are other ways of communicating.

Maja was a little over two, and David was between nine and ten. We were courageous to adopt at our age, and they showed their character by adjusting to the "old folks." However, we lost no time in teaching them to swim in the lovely Marmara Sea, to play tennis, "beyzbal," and what we could not teach them they learned in the American School where they were enrolled very soon after arrival. The first party David attended he wore his "leder hosen" and was the envy of all the American and Turkish kids. (Amazing, isn't it, how quickly the young break down barriers?) In a year's time both David and Maja became one of the gang, speaking English as well as any. We were careful, however, to see that they did not abandon their German culture. In Istanbul at that time were many refugees from Germany and they kept alive our childrens' interest in the best of Germany.

The Germans in Turkey were the most admired of all nationalities and Americans were a close second, so the children were accepted from the outset. The staff and students at the Dershane "adopted" them right off, patiently taught them Turkish and advised us how to raise them. David, in a burst of gallantry, delighted Maja by taking her along when he played "cops and robbers" with the kids in the neighborhood. Our children could play in the ancient Hippodrome nearby, in storied castles from the days when Istanbul was called Byzantium, or Constantinople. Not far away was an ancient aquaduct, then the Blue Mosque (height of Muslim architecture) and the Sancta Sophia Church, later a mosque and now a museum. It was not only fun but living history, experiences they have cherished through the years. But more important was that they were making friends with many nationalities in their play.

One day, while the children were exploring castles along the Bosphorous I found Maja crying because she had been left behind by the boys, and her brother had gotten tired of helping her over the walls too high even for a tomboy. I said, "Maja, you are just as smart as they are, you use that good head of yours, and you'll win." The next day the boys were all setting their pace to Maja's and showing quite a concern for her. "What happened?" I asked a delighted girl. "They are playing history and I am their nurse," she replied archly. She and David have always had great courage. I remember watching her and David marching off to school during the 1958 Revolution in Lebanon. One would never have thought there was danger, but I noticed David was very protective although some of the other boys thought him a sissy for being so attentive to a girl. In their society girls did not always rate as high as boys.

Through the eyes, minds and hearts of our two dear children we were able to see life in the Middle East in a different persepctive. The people there have a great love for their children and older people, and our two children brought us closer to Turkish and Lebanese families.

Every year at Christmas we invited the staff from the Dershane and their families for a party around our tree. There were little gifts for the children, a homemade "crech" and singing. There were Muslims and Christians and Jews at our party. The first Christmas that the children were with us was unforgettable. The staff surprised us a few months later when we were invited to their homes for "Sheker Bayram" (their sugar holiday) when they celebrated the end of Ramadan with feasting and gifts. We all found harmony and unity during those celebrations. Afterwards David said, "I never thought there could be so much love anywhere." Nor did we.

FROM BLUE BEAD TO MODERN MEDICINE

Some Westerners are astonished to learn that medicine really originated, for the most part, with the Arabs. The Moors (a mixture of Arabs and Berbers) who migrated from what is now the Middle East and North Africa to Spain in the eighth century, brought with them a rather sophisticated medical science. As a matter of fact, certain historians point out that when Europe was agonizing through the Middle Ages (476 to 1,000 A.D.) and medical practice was quite primitive on that continent, invaders brought back medical knowledge from Spain which was considerably ahead of that in the rest of Europe. If one has lived in the Middle East, one remembers that the use of herbs, gums of trees and foods like cheese have been widely utilized in treatment of the ill since early Arab times. Even today, herbs are still used in many countries of the world in modern medicine.

It is said that while Florence Nightingale treated the wounded and sick from the Crimean War (1854-56) in her makeshift hospital on the Bosphorous, a Turkish herbalist tried several times to see her and tell her of his remarkable cures with herbs. Her assistants thought him a charlatan and would not let him visit Miss Nightingale. However, one day she met him quite by chance and he opened up a new area of medical treatment for diseases. It is further stated that Miss Nightingale benefitted from the herbalist in the sensitive treatment of wounds with certain herbs and gums.

Nurse Nightingale became the prototype for nursing. Before her time, both in England and in America nurses were often ignorant and sometimes sadistic. Even in my mother's day, she was one of few girls of prominent families to go into nursing; in fact, her father, a country doctor near Pittsburgh, was so upset with her decision to serve as a nurse that he questioned her intelligence.

The early discoveries of the Arabs spread throughout the Middle East and we benefit today from their knowledge. While visiting in Turkey, Syria and Lebanon, we often stayed in villages so remote that the people were practically free of most diseases. Dr. Cyril Haas, missionary doctor in Adana, Turkey for many years observed four things that kept the people reasonably healthy: one, the ubiquitous sun; two, the cologne sprinkled on the hands of guests; three, the herbs and natural foods and; four, the gums from trees used to prevent tooth decay. (A dentist would have some difficulty making a living in the villages.) Among the favorite foods are goat's milk, yogurt, mutton, grapes, honey, figs and certain berries. Nor are there many preservatives. The favorite is salt. In our travels in areas where one could go only by horseback, we found it not unusual for people to be in their 90s and 100s. I must hasten to stress the point that the above facts do not take anything from the reality that the people do sometimes desperately need medical care. Trachoma, typhus, dysentery, yellow jaundice and some social diseases (mainly in the large towns and cities), goiters and malaria (the latter has been stamped out pretty largely) and of course childbirth and childrens' diseases. Evelyn Kyle Kalchas in her recent book "Food From the Fields," speaks of the medicinal use of herbs frequently.

Early in the Turkey years, I learned more and more about the "blue bead" and how it could ward off disease and evil spirits. For example, one never admired a baby without immediately saying, "May the evil eye not touch him, or her." Few children in the rural areas are without a string of blue beads, either across their foreheads, around their necks, or their wrists. Since the people sometimes mistrust injections and certain medicines, the doctors would insert medicines in candy blue beads and dispense them to the children. This was particularly true in the case of malaria where quinine was used. Some of us from the West carried quinine with us in the early days.

Dr. Shepard of Aintab, a pioneer Medical Missionary whose son and grandson followed him in Turkey, used to say, "I have learned never to underestimate the power of the blue bead, nor the faith of the people in it." It is a curious coincidence that both Dr. Haas and Dr. Shepard had names which meant a great deal to the people whom they treated, for Haas means "the perfect one," and Shepard means "a leader."

The blue bead is also used in unexpected places and situations. Once near the Cilician Gates in the Taurus Mountains I rode in an old Buick with one of the most reckless drivers anyone ever encountered. After taking his third sharp curve on the wrong side of the road, I asked him, "Have you ever had an accident?" "No," he assured me, taking both hands off the steering wheel to dramatize his good fortune, "so long as I have the blue beads on my radiator and Allah in the seat beside me what harm can there be?"

Perhaps one of the greatest contributions made by the medical missionaries was that they gave dignity and competence to the nursing profession. The nurses training centers established throughout Turkey under the American Board of the Congregational Church trained young women of different nationalities and religions as nurses. At the outset the nurses were mainly Christian since no Muslim girl of good family would dare to go into this field where up to that time the nurses, except for the Christian girls, were uneducated and of lower class.

However, under the New Republic the women were able to discard the veil and were freed to have higher education. Then a few Muslim girls chose nuring as a career. From the first they proved to be competent. Bayan Fahrinissa Seden, a Muslim and a pioneer in the profession, did her undergraduate work in Turkey, then studied nursing in Detroit. On her return to Istanbul, she established a school of nursing where Muslim girls came for training. One story is told of a wealthy Turkish father who finally became reconciled to his daughter's becoming a nurse, but sent a servant to the hospital with her to empty the bedpans.

The greatest prejudice for Muslim nursing girls to overcome was when they had to serve men patients, even though the men were partially clothed. Moreover, few women entering nursing could find husbands willing to marry one who had been, or was a nurse. Florence Nightingale, the "Lady with the Lamp," lighted the way to future generations of Muslim women of courage and concern for the sick and today many of those women serve in hospitals and clinics of the Middle East. American nurses and doctors and many other foreign doctors and nurses deserve great credit for these reforms. But so do Kemal Ataturk and his Government, as well as open-minded Turkish doctors, who often supported the nursing profession at great risk to their careers. It is entirely fitting that an Anglican Church has been dedicated as the Florence Nighingale Memorial Church. On the Centenary occasion tributes from many nations were paid to Miss Nightingale.

Adana hospital nurses in village dress in 1934 in
the Taurus Mountains, Turkey.

THE HOJA SAYS

Early in my studies in Turkish, the teacher introduced me to the "Nasrettin Hoja" stories. The Hoja (hoe-jaw), a combination of Muslim priest and schoolteacher, was a kind of Paul Bunyan of the Middle East. One finds his stories told widely in the Middle East but sometimes under different names. In his village of Ak Shehir, Turkey, the Hoja lived with his wife and donkey. He was known for his wit and wisdom and for his tall tales. The Hoja's final gesture of independence and disdain of authority is found on the edge of town, a very simple grave with a padlocked gate in front, but no fence or walls. He had left his humor as a bequest to his friends and as a final insult to the Sultan.

Our children loved the Hoja and his little donkey. They would say at bedtime, "Daddy, tell us another Hoja story." It seemed they would never have enough. In fact, many stories attributed to the Hoja may not have been his at all, but I tapped them anyway.

Here's one: The Hoja bowed to no man and stood in awe of no man. About 1400 A.D., Tamerlane, who had heard about the Hoja, sent for him to come to his encampment on the edge of Ak Shehir thinking to put this village rustic in his place. But little did he realize the craftiness and ingenuity of the little wise man. Of course, from what he had heard of the Hoja's fame, Tamerlane already had a grudging respect for him. The Conqueror decided it might be wise to have the Hoja on his side before invading the village.

True to character, the Hoja refused the horse offered by his host to go to the audience. Instead he rode to the encampment on his beloved donkey. In the Conqueror's presence the usual formality of bowing was dispensed with and the Hoja would not sit on the chair assigned to him which was slightly lower than the throne of Tamerlane. Instead the visitor sat on a cushion usually reserved for the court jester. Tamerlane's plan to downgrade the Hoja before his followers failed because the Hoja's entire mien and mood was not one of subjection, but a mix of dignity and independence. The entire audience continued in this vein.

The truth was that the Conqueror was so pleased with the man that he sent a gift of an elephant to Ak Shehir. But the town was small and very poor, and the elephant was very large and very hungry. At first the villagers were very honored by the gift saying "Mashallah" (what a miracle!), Tamerlane was going to invade our town, but instead he sent a gift. This is the Hoja's doing. What a great man he is!" But they began to cool toward the Hoja because the elephant ate so much of the food that they, themselves, became very hungry. As usual, when in trouble they went to the Hoja for advice. The Hoja thought longer than usual, then said, "Let's form a committee about the elephant, meet tomorrow morning after the 'Namaz' (morning prayer) at the village well and then have an audience with His Excellency." While the villagers all agreed on the strategy, the Hoja was the only one who showed up at the well, so for the Hoja, nothing was left but for him to go alone to the Conqueror, thank him for the elephant, saying, "Our people liked your gift so much they desire a second elephant!"

Some of the Hoja stories were of only local interest. Once the Hoja's neighbor, whom he disliked and tried to avoid, came to borrow the Hoja's donkey. "It is so sad," the Hoja mourned, "Last night my donkey died," It seemed to be on cue, for at that very moment, the donkey brayed very loudly from his stall. The neighbor was indignant and accused the Hoja, "Efendi, I am surprised with you, our Priest and Teacher, that you would lie like this." The Hoja replied, "Whom do you believe, my donkey or me?"

A third kind of story was similar to the rather grim tales of the East European underground during the war. So, among the villagers in the days of the sultans when almost every third man was a spy, humor was the only option left for getting even with the Sultan. Now near Ak Shehir was a natural pond where the Hoja loved to fish. When he was angry with the Sultan he used to say, "A dying fish smells first from the head," He thought of this again, and conceived a subtle plan to get even with the Sultan. The Sultan's spies and advisors realizing that they were missing a good thing by not putting a high tax on fishing, decided that their local spy should look into the matter. At the same time the Hoja was very shrewd in inviting the local government official, whom he knew to be a spy, to fish with him. The villagers, briefed by the Hoja, also showed up in advance of the Hoja and his guest and began to fish. But as fast as they caught their fish, they would unhook them, leaving the smelly fish on the shore. Eventually the spy, a rather dainty little man, put a handkerchief to his nose for the odor of dying fish was unbearable. After all, the local spy was a very simple fellow so he saw no connection between the Head of the Empire and the head of the fish.

In due course the spy reported to his superior at the palace that it was indeed true and the villagers were referring to the fish, and not to the Sultan, when they spoke the parable of the fish. But in the Sultan's Saray the more sophisticated observed, "The Hoja has outwitted us again!" To the delight of the village of Ak Shehir, the tax on fish was never levied.

When the foreigner learns the Turkish language and understands the Turkish humor, he is accepted. One way you know that you are accepted is when people will tell you about your "faux pas" in their language and customs. Some charming stories are told about foreigners and their Turkish. An American diplomat had newly arrived in Istanbul and asked his secretary where he might hear the best Turkish spoken. She advised, "Ride on the Bosphorous boats next to the ladies section and there you will hear the most elegant Turkish." The advice was taken and the diplomat learned quite a few phrases. Later, in comparing with another Turk he said, "Turkchem, nasil buliyorsunuz, my friend?" (How do you find my Turkish?) The friend replied, "Why Hanim Efendi (Madame), I like it very much."

My Turkish teacher and other friends saw to it that I learned some of the poetry and parables which are a rich and relevant part of the language. When you do a good deed for somebody and receive no appreciation for it, it will be a comfort to remember this saying:

> "Do good, and throw it into the Sea; if the fish
> doesn't recognize it, God (Allah) will."

Or if you are crafty remember this one:

> "The bear is your uncle until you get across the bridge."

(This was used in meeting the Russian threat.)

Once on the Orient Express in the 1930s I found myself in a second class compartment with a middle-class Turkish family. Although I had brought food with me, the family insisted that I share their meal. During the dinner they asked the three inevitable questions: "How old are you? What is your salary? Are you married?" It must not be thought as impudence, but a natural curiosity. When I admitted to being single they all looked sad and the Grandmother — who had no doubt helped to arrange a good many marriages — observed, "Yazuk (what a pity!), couldn't your family afford to buy you a wife??" That was in the 1930s when I was still single. In the cities today, arranged marriages are rather rare, but in many villages the custom still continues.

Kurdish mother and child. The woman is dressed in
traditional wedding costume. (Aleppo)

CHILDS' PLAY and PUBLIC RELATIONS

All of the time that our children were with us in the Middle East they were a credit to Germany, to us and to their adopted country, the United States. Just as the new German authorities had given us every facility in their adoption, our own Consulate speeded up the process so that from the time when they arrived in Turkey they were a part of the family and had American privileges. By the same token the Turkish authorities went out of their way to process the childrens' papers quickly.

Without David and Maja we would not have had the measure of joy, adventure and friendship that they brought to us. Love, of course, came later and it has been genuine. We have always tried to let them be natural and free. At the outset we believed that the decision to live in the "Old City" of Istanbul was a good introduction to the Middle East. Here they learned the language, customs and qualities of the people. Much sooner than we had been able to do, they became acquainted with shopkeepers, policemen, "Hamals" (porters in the streets), teachers and university students, tramway conductors, Dershane members and the kids in the neighborhood. David's Turkish was precise and correct, and Maja's was charming; the Turks loved to hear them talk Turkish!

A Sunday adventure that David had soon after they arrived from Germany stands out in our memory. David has always been a methodical, well-organized individual with an underlying affection for people. He is curious about what motivates people and this curiosity led him to explore the covered Bazaar, the teeming life of the Galata Bridge and the 1,000 underground columns beneath Saint Sophia. He also loved to travel in the Jeep to out-of-the-way places.

Apparently it was this same curiosity that made David disappear one Sunday, and it was unusual for him not to tell us where he was going or when he would return. Finally, Maja and I went to look for him. Not far from home we noticed a large crowd at the corner of "Alemdar" (Leader Avenue) and our own street "Belediye" (Municipal Place). So intent were the people on watching something we could not see that they were unusually quiet. The traffic was almost at a standstill; the ever-raucous horns silent. Maja was the first to see David, who seemed to be the center of interest. With all of the dignity of a ten year old David was mounted on a barrel in the middle of Alemdar Avenue, directing traffic as if he were in downtown Munich. His exaggerated gestures had captivated the crowd, affecting even the traffic cop whom he had replaced. Although vehicles had slowed to a crawl, David was giving directions as if everything were normal. Soon, the inevitable photographer and reporter appeared. For as long as we stayed in Istanbul the Turkish traffic cops were imitating the German gestures. We did not discourage David in this public relations venture, because it was an education for him and for the people.

As we left, David had a warm handshake from the traffic cop and the crowd gave their approval with "Mashallahs" (what wonders Allah has wrought) and "Yaman bir Chocuk" (that is some boy!). Needless to say, the next day he was a hero in his school.

Maja had her high adventure in Beirut, Lebanon under more serious circumstances. On the day of her big moment my wife and I had gone to Tripoli in North Lebanon on YMCA business and had returned late that night. Maja had been left with our Lebanese maid where we thought she would be safe. She was then about ten years old.

As soon as we opened our apartment door we guessed there was something wrong with our daughter because the maid, who was very fond of both children, was making wild gestures and speaking incoherently in Arabic, French and German. She finally told us that Maja was in trouble, but she was too excited to be specific. At last she said, "Maja is in her room and she needs her mother." Mother was no sooner in the room when Maja blurted out, "Mom, I have been arrested."!

We were so relieved that she was home safe that the word "arrested" slipped our attention. Soon the whole story came out. By this time David had joined us and Maja smiled for the first time and gloated, "David, I did something you have never done." She had that 'getting-even' gleam in her eye.

The 1958 Lebanese Revolution was tapering off, but security was still strict in the city. And it was especially strict in our neighborhood because the Foreign Secretary, Charles Malik, and the Prime Minister lived nearby. The rebels were still trying to capture members of the Chamoun Cabinet and one could hear sporadic shooting, especially at night. Maja was restless, so she was glad when her playmates — a mix of nationalities — appeared so they could go out. The kids had harmless toy guns and they were playing "cops and robbers." Maja, the only girl, had to have a toy pistol too, so she bought one at a nearby toy shop. Just as she was loading the gun a security Jeep came roaring around the corner, grabbed Maja and one of the boys and almost threw them into their vehicle. The men from Security Patrol then made off with the kids without a word of explanation. The boys did not know it, but where they had just been shooting caps was near the Prime Minister's home. The shooting was loud enough for the Prime Minister to think it might be the real thing, so not knowing it was childs' play he immediately ordered the arrest of the "gunmen." His anger and anxiety were understandable.

There was no opportunity for Maja to tell anybody at home about the arrest, so she and the boy who was now crying, sat in the Jeep, crowded in between two grim and heavily armed guards. It was like a nightmare, or a horror movie, but when they turned a corner and stopped in front of the "Karakol" (precinct police station) they knew it was for real.

Meanwhile, back in our neighborhood another scenario was unfolding. Our local grocer saw the Jeep careening around the corner with the guards holding the kids at gunpoint and spunky Maja waving her arms in protest. The grocer ran to tell our maid, the maid called the boy's mother, and the mother called the American Embassy, which we, with our penchant for working with the people of the country, regretted. Our maid and the grocer then went to the Karakol where, after taking a good look at the kids, the police became less hostile. The next morning the Chief of the Karakol said, "That's a brave, wonderful girl. She did not cry once." But Maja was shaken, and we felt it might have been worse. The next day the newspapers helped everybody save face when it reported that some misguided American youth had fired some toy guns near the Prime Minister's home, but Security had apprehended them in time. The following morning a Lebanese neighbor called us on the phone and said, "What a courageous little girl. But I hope you will not punish her."

The interior of an Arab home, Aleppo, Syria in 1933.

THE EGYPTIAN CONNECTION

"Time is running out for the moderates in reaching a peace settlement for the Middle East," wrote a friend once high up in the councils of Egypt. Having been in Egypt many times during our twenty years in the Middle East, I am convinced that of all the Arab nations Egypt is perhaps our best hope for marshalling the moderates for a settlement. Moreover, if we cannot or will not listen to the moderates both in Israel and in Egypt, then we may see the extremists on both sides take the initiative. As I write this chapter, it is rumored that the parties to the present negotiation will reconvene soon; it is devoutly hoped that they may meet and have a meeting of minds on some of the basic issues. If, as some believe, the settlements on the West Bank of the Jordan are the main issue, then one remembers and applauds what one distinguished Israeli leader said some years ago, "Peace is more important than real estate."

Almost since the partition of Palestine, the Israeli leaders have been insisting that they want to meet with the Arab leaders to work out an agreement and build a peace. It seems to those of us who have lived and worked in that area that the proof of that statement is long overdue. I believe that it has been nothing short of a miracle that Anwar Sadat was able to visit Israel and that both sides were willing to sit down together in Egypt and at Camp David. The "hopes and fears of many years" were caught up in those meetings. Whatever one's politics, one cannot help but praise President Carter, Cyrus Vance and their colleagues for bringing off these meetings. We came very close to agreement as a result of those encounters and I believe both Israel and Egypt should be commended for them. It seemed, to a relative outsider, that the moderate voices were heard in those meetings.

I would like also to express my conviction that until the question of a Palestinian homeland is solved, there will be no lasting peace in the Middle East. When one comes to know the moderate Palestinians as we did from working closely with them in the refugee camps, in non-political relief, and rehabilitation services through the Voluntary Agencies and the UNRWA (United Nations Refugee Work Agency), one learns that they are worthwhile and one believes that their cause is just. I can still see in memory, the troubled and anxious face of a 19 year old Palestinian youth in one of the camps at Jericho as he said to me, "I have never known a land I could call my own and I have dreamed of returning to Palestine all my life. Why should our people, who had nothing to do with the persecution of the Jews in Europe, have to suffer homelessness all these years to give them a haven. In spite of the fact that we are refugees, many of our people have a compassion for the Jewish people, for our parents remember what good neighbors we were with them in the happier days in Palestine." At the time of this talk, the young man was a student in the YMCA Vocational School in Jericho. He is now working in Kuwait.

Quoting again from our confidential source in Egypt, he wrote, "We must take the risk of including Palestinian representatives among the negotiators for until we do they are going to be outsiders, and opponents, of any solution our side might propose."

Some believe that the only hold that Egypt has over the other Arab States is military, that without the involvement of the Egyptian forces, the Arab forces, no matter how united, would be inadequate to meet Israel. This may be true militarily, but there are many other respects in which Egypt can make significant connections with the Arab States, for the Arab States respect the culture and quality of the Egyptians, their long history of diplomacy and their profound religious tradition. I think it is safe to say that Egypt, since the Revolution in 1953 has, for the most part been a moderate and constructive force in that region of the world. During President Anwar Sadat's visit to Israel, Prime Minister Menachem Begin's statement that President Sadat represented an ancient and justifiably proud nation can still stand the test, and one only hopes that the euphoria of that visit can be translated into something more than rhetoric.

When we focus on the human condition and the human values in that part of the globe, further conflict is unthinkable. If our aim is to stress the positive, the people of that part of the human family have much in common. They are both Semites; both have a religion that stresses justice and human rights; both speak languages which have much in common; and both have more to gain than to lose in the forging of a lasting peace. Furthermore, if the rich gifts each has to bring to a unified region can be put into play, the Middle East could be a model for a world which needs one so badly. Finally, one must not neglect the contributions of mind, heart and spirit which the other Arab people could bring to such an alignment.

Beduin sisters in Aleppo in 1933.

KHALIL GIBRAN, POET and PRAGMATIST

"His power came from some great reservoir of spiritual life else it could not have been so universal and so potent, but the majesty and beauty of the language with which he clothed it were all his own."

— Claude Bragdon

On the winding road between Tripoli, in North Lebanon, and the famed Cedars of Lebanon is a small village, Becharre, perched on a precipice from which one can look down thousands of feet to the Sacred River (The Kadisha). It was here, in this mountain place of myth and mystery, that Khalil Gibran, the poet, was born and grew up as a boy and young man.

In his ancestral home they would show you his study, hanging precariously over a precipice, where he began to write "The Prophet" at the age of seventeen. It is said that the work, one of his greatest in the minds of critics, was completed ten years later when he was 27, and that he wrote it 71 times before he was satisfied. The book was published in 1923.

Among the Arab people nothing is so beloved or moving as poetry, and the poetry and art of Gibran are favorites. But Gibran's fame and following went beyond the Middle East to almost every part of the world. He was particularly popular in the United States among people of all ages and still is so. "The Prophet" now in its 79th printing is widely read by high school and college youth even today; perhaps this is evidence of its universality.

Whenever his works or those of many other Middle Eastern poets are recited or read over the radio or on television, crowds come to listen with rapture, like crowds attend athletic events in the United States. Perhaps Gibran's appeal is profound because his life had such heights and depths; he was indeed a man of joys and sorrows.

Early in his youth he fell in love with a lovely Lebanese girl. However, their love was never to be fulfilled for her father, against his will but bound by the marriage customs of those days, was forced to agree to her marriage to a far lesser man chosen by the patriarch of their church. The trauma of this experience, for both the girl and Gibran is dramatically told in Gibran's book, "Broken Wings." After this experience, Khalil's bitterness against the church grew and he entered a very pragmatic period in his thought and writings.

Without taking sides in this growing controversy between the poet and the church, one must point out that the church (in this case Maronite Catholic) of Gibran, like many sects in the Middle East was deeply involved in politics. It was just assumed that the church leaders, and particularly the patriarchs would have both a spiritual and a political role in the country. In fact in addition to their spiritual services which are often considerable, they often had a significant role in troubled times in reconciling various political factions. This was particularly true during the 1958 revolution in Lebanon. Hence, when one of the patriarchs was campaigning for reappointment he wrote to Gibran in America asking for his support. Knowing of Gibran's broad influence over the minds and hearts of the Lebanese he thought that Gibran's endorsement would weigh heavily in his campaign. Gibran's reply was immediate and down-to-earth. He cabled an angry "no" to the request. Naturally this move was, perhaps, not wise but it was honest and widened the breach.

On the other hand one cannot read Gibran without realizing the depth and breadth of his spirit and the reality of his faith. He was, like many creative spirits, far ahead of his times and a living example of a "prophet without honor in his own country." Now there is a resurgence of interest in Gibran, as evidenced in wider sales of his works, and of the loving care by his friends and the government of Lebanon of his tomb on the mountainside above his birthplace. It was my privilege to visit that sacred place several times with my friend, David Karam, a Lebanese, and an authority on the man and his writings. As we gazed down at the Sacred River and up to his village near The Cedars of Lebanon David spoke of some of the poems inspired by the beauty and meaning of those hills and valleys. At that moment, this place became a shrine for both of us. In that vast silence the words, so relevant to Gibran, came to mind, "We shall not see his likes again."

Bab-Ul-Hadid or Gate of the Moon in Aleppo, 1933.

BAALBEK — (Heliopolis) — City of the Sun

The ancient seafaring Phoenicians (about 1200 B.C.) built harbors and city-states along the Lebanese coast and in northern Syria on the present site of Baalbek, they created a temple to Baal. Hence the name Baalbek. Later the Greeks called it Heliopolis, City of the Sun. Perhaps it is a blessing that the Romans and the Arabs, who came later, did not add to the confusion with their own nomenclature.

Baalbek, now within the Republic of Lebanon, is one of the best preserved of the ancient cities in the Middle East in spite of earthquakes, wars, revolutions, occupation and the inroads of looters. Perhaps its survival could be credited to the Syrians and the French. The latter ruled Syria and what is now Lebanon through a mandate. Also credit is due German archaeologists and those of other nations as well as Lebanese archaeologists who, until recent revolutions, have done much to restore the city to its former grandeur.

Baalbek nestles between the Lebanon and anti-Lebanon Mountains at the northern end of the fertile Beqaa (Beka) Valley. On either side of Baalbek the land rises into the foothills of the Lebanon Ranges, so that from almost any point one can see "The City of the Sun." Most spectacular of its landmarks and seen from great distances are the six towering columns of the Temple of Jupiter, which are all the more impressive because they stand alone.

In his 24th edition of the "History of Baalbek" (1956), ex-Curator of the Ruins of Baalbek, Michel M. Alouf, distinguished archaeologist, sets the stage for a study of Baalbek and its surroundings. In his foreword, Professor Alouf pays tribute to the Germans and French Missions working at Baalbek and concludes with this observation:

> Baalbek! City of the Gods, chosen home of the Sun-worshippers — City of the Sun, which is the essence of all life, venerated by the Greeks and the Romans and admired by all nations. What more can be added to its glory? Naught but to chant again its beauties. And this attempt has been made by one of Baalbek's children — one who loves her dearly. May the admirers of Baalbek ever increase.!

Each year in peacetime, more and more tourists have visited Baalbek and almost without exception they have left as admirers of the modern town as well as the ancient city. Baalbek is not only a tourist center but a center of culture and pageantry. Each summer there are concerts, folklore programs and historical pageants which attract people from throughout the Middle East and beyond. Among distinguished guest artists, Leonard Bernstein was perhaps the most appreciated as he gave a series of concerts with his orchestra to sellout crowds in the Temple of Jupiter. The outdoor setting with the luminous light of a summer evening lends itself to great music and great drama. Lebanese friends with us the evening of Bernstein's performance remarked that they had never witnessed such an ovation. Mr. Bernstein was called back time and again. The spectacular views of the fertile Valley of Be-qaa, with the Lebanese Mountains on either side and the Temples of Venus, Bacchus and Jupiter as inspiration made that evening unforgettable.

Perhaps not many know that the surrounding countryside is roughly equivalent to "the land flowing in milk and honey" mentioned in the Bible. Again, Professor Alouf describes the character and the fertility of the land:

> There were sufficient reasons to cause Baalbek to become one of the richest and most prosperous towns of Syria. Situated in a fertile and well-watered region, the town overlooks a vast plain, which produces the best grain and most delicious fruits. The plain is surrounded by high mountains covered with cypress, cedar, pine, oak, juniper, and terebinth forests (yielding turpentine), where large flocks of goats and sheep graze. . . Beside this, Baalbek occupied an important strategic position among the most important towns of those days, situated at a distance of two days journey from Tripoli, Jebeil (ancient Byblos), Beirut, Sidon, Damascus and Homs. . . It became an important center, a market frequented by caravans, business men and dealers from all countries, who exported their products to distant regions.

The hospitality and friendliness of the population of the modern city, even in troubled times, has impressed many visitors. We took a visiting party of Americans to Baalbek for a weekend during the 1958 revolution. While we and our Lebanese hosts were aware of the violence in parts of the country, Baalbek was surprisingly peaceful during that visit. Again, as we had on many occasions, we experienced the warm welcome and warmer hospitality of the Alouf brothers at the Palmyra Hotel built upon the ruins of the ancient theater of the city. Indeed the managers saw to it that we had the best of care, including a balcony with a stunning view of the six columns of the Temple of Jupiter. The leisurely pace of the town, and the people helped us to forget for the moment the world's unrest.

As usual, the Lebanese merchants of silks, rare rugs, jewelry and pottery were eager for trade, as had been many of their Phoenician ancestors, but they were also anxious to tell us in almost perfect English about their relatives in California, Illinois and New York. As a matter of fact, there are more persons of Lebanese background living outside the country than inside. As one travels in this small country with its great beauty of mountains, fields and the sea, one can understand why it is called the "Switzerland of the Middle East." And one hopes that when peace comes again to Lebanon it may again become a Mecca for visitors and a delight to the eye and heart.

THE MEVLIDI SHERIF

Lyman MacCallum, representative for the British-American Bible Society and well-known scholar in the Turkish language, history and culture is the translator of the Birth-Song of the Prophet, "The Mevlidi Sherif," written in the latter part of the 14th century by Suleyman Chelebi, famed Turkish poet. Lyman and I were colleagues when I served in Turkey; his knowledge of the Turkish language and the Islamic religion and culture was very helpful to me as I endeavored to understand and appreciate the Middle East and its people. One day Lyman said to some of us, "There are four things the Turkish people place above everything else: the religion of Islam, poetry, Ataturk, and their honor. In the Birth-Song of the Prophet, both religion and poetry (set to music) are found and considered sacred.

On the cover of "Birth-Song" these introductory words are written:

In the days of Tamerlane (at the end of the 14th Century) Suleyman Chelebi was one of the royal chaplains of Sultan Beyazid, the Thunderbolt. When Tamerlane overthrew Beyazid, Suleyman found refuge as chief-priest of the Great Mosque at Bursa (First capital of the Ottoman Empire). There he composed the MEVLIDI SHERIF, to confute a teaching that Muhammed was no greater than other Prophets. The poem survives after 500 years and is much loved by the people of Turkey. It is recited at times of thanksgiving and sorrow and on many special occasions. An authority on Turkey said recently, "No one can know what Mohammed means to a Turk unless he is familiar with this poem."

The poem consists of a number of sections or cantos, usually separated by a couplet and response which serve as chorus. The sections are:

I. A song of invocation and praise to Allah.
II. A brief request for prayers for the author, "Suleyman the lowly."
III. A discourse on the Light of Muhammed, or the prophetic succession.
IV. The Birth of Muhammed.
V. The "Merhaba", a triumphal chorus of welcome to the new-born Prophet
VI. Further recital of the marvels attending the birth.
VII. The miracles of the Prophet.
VIII. The "Miradj", or heavenly journey of the Prophet.
IX. Concluding confession and prayer.

Quoting again from Mr. MacCallum's preface to his translation:

In Republican Turkey the Mevlid continues to be chanted in mosques and in homes, and the recital takes place either on some religious festival, such as the Night of Power, or at a time of rejoicing, such as a house-warming or a victory of Turkish arms, or in a time of mourning. Perhaps its commonest occurrence is on the fortieth day after a death; in-

vitations to such memorial recitals are a common feature of
the Istanbul press. During the recital rose-water is sprinkled
on the hands of the congregation, and sweets are
distributed.

The fact that the Mevlidi Sherif, as the finest expression of
reverence for Muhammed, forms an essential part in the
religious pattern of most Turkish minds, and that from its
striking pictures and musical lines many Turks draw a large
part of their stock of religious ideas, may give this poem interest and significance even for many who have little direct
contact with the world of Islam. Remembering what the
music of Christmas carols means to the Western world may
help to an understanding of what the Turk experiences as
he listens to the music of Suleyman Chelebi's Mevlidi Sherif.

The following gives the complete section on "The Birth of Muhammed"
(on whom be peace!):

"Now Amine, Muhammed's tender mother
(Mother-of-pearl, her one pearl like none other).

Had been with child by Abdullah, the faithful,
And time had sped, her hour was fast approaching.

But in the night when he to earth descended,
A host of herald signs bespoke his coming.

It was the happy month, Rebi-ul-evel, (Spring-the 3rd lunar month)
And of this month the twelfth, Isneyn, the Blessed,

On which was born the Welfare of the Peoples,
'Mid marvels by his wond'ring mother witnessed.

"I saw," said she, "wondrous light upspringing,
And streaming from my house, with blaze increasing.

Round it the sun revolved, moth-like and dazzled,
While earth and sky gave back this matchless splendor.

Heaven's radiant doors stood wide, and Dark was vanquished,
There came three angels bearing shining banners;

They raised one at the world's east brink, another
At farthest west, the third atop the Kaaba.

Then rank on rank the heavenly host descended,
And round my dwelling marched, as 'twere God's mansion.

This multitude made clear to me that straightway
Their lord to earth would come, to bless his people.

In air I saw a silken mattress wafted,
By angel band adoringly attended

So clear before my eyes appeared these visions,
That all my heart o'erflowed with glowing wonder.

But now the wall at hand was sharply riven;
In stepped three shining houris* fresh from Heaven.

Some say that one was Asiye, fair consort
Of Egypt's King, who noble Moses nurtured.

One was, without a doubt the Lady Mary;
The third, a graceful houri, their attendant.

Most graciously the moon-browed three approached me,
And, bowing low, said kindly: 'Peace be on thee!'

Then close at hand they sat in friendly circle
While each announced glad tidings of Mustafa.

To me they said: 'Not since the world's creation
Hath mother had such cause for exultation.

No son like thine, such strength and grace possessing,
Hath God to earth sent down for its redressing.

Great favour hast thou found, thou lovely mother,
To bear a son surpassing every other.

Sultan is he, all hidden truth possessing,
Full knowledge of Unity professing.

For love of him, they son, the skies are turning;
Mankind and angels for his face are yearning.

This is the night foretold in song and story,
In which the worlds rejoice to see his glory.

This night the world a paradise he maketh,
This night God's mercy on mankind awaketh.

Men of goodwill this night are all elated,
All upright men this night have long awaited.

The mercy of both Worlds is he, Mustafa,
The refuge of the sinner is Mustafa!'

* Angelic, heavenly beings.

With gracious words his nature they pictured,
And for that blessed Radiance set me yearning.

Here Amine made ending, for the hour
In which should come that best of men had sounded."

"I thirst," she cried, "I thirst, I burn with fever!"
A brimming glass to her at once was proffered.

White was that glass, than snow more white, and colder;
No sweetmeat ever made held half such sweetness.

"I drank it, and my being filled with glory,
Nor could I longer self from light distinguish.

On pinions bright a bird of white came floating,
And stroked my back, so strongly yet how kindly;

The Sultan of the Faith that hour was given,
And drowned in glory lay both earth and heaven."

Now pray to him, make peace and full submission,
That Paradise be yours for your contrition.

If from Hell's flame you hope to find salvation,
With love and zeal repeat the Salutation."

Response

Blessing and greeting upon thee, O Apostle of Allah!
Blessing and greeting upon thee, O Beloved of Allah!

All things created joyfully acclaimed him,
Sorrow was done, new life the world was flooding.

The very atoms joined in mighty chorus,
Crying with sweetest voices: Welcome, welcome!

Welcome, O matchless Sultan, thou art welcome.
Welcome, O Source of Knowledge, thou art welcome.

Welcome, thou Secret of the Koran, welcome,
Welcome, Affliction's Cure, thou art most welcome.

Welcome, thou Nightingale of Beauty's garden,
Welcome, to him who knows the Lord of Pardon.

Welcome, thou Moon and Sun of God's salvation.
Welcome, who knowest from Truth no deviation.

Welcome, the rebel's only place of hiding,
Welcome, the poor man's only sure confiding.

Welcome, Abiding Spirit, thou art welcome,
Welcome, the Lovers' Cup-bearer, O Welcome.

Welcome, thou Eyesight of thy true adorer,
Welcome, thou Prince, loved by the World's Restorer.

Welcome, the humble soul's Illuminator,
Welcome, thou cherished Friend of the Creator   . . . .

Welcome, thou Monarch by two worlds awaited,
For whom both earth and heaven were created.

O Thou, whose face with noonday spendour gloweth,
Whose hand is quick to raise up all the fallen.

O balm of broken hearts, joy of the contrite,
O Sultan of the world and all its creatures.

O thou, Belov'd of God, grant thy assistance,
Smile on us in that hour when ends existence.   . . . .

(At this point the congregation stands to welcome the arrival of the Prophet.
The attributes of the Prophet, and of Allah, follow with some repetition.)

Seljuk Mosque, Ceserea in 1932.

THE BOSPHOROUS BOATS
A SAGA OF THE SEA

Istanbul is indeed a city "where men go down to the sea in ships." There is scarcely a moment of the day of night when there is not some movement in the waters of the Bosphorous, the Golden Horn and the Marmara Sea, names which bring nostalgia, memories of adventure, wars and conquests and the pleasure of travel in peacetime. In a broader sense one's imagination transcends the local scene, however unique and beautiful to the Dardenelles, the Aegean, the Mediterranean and the Adriatic to the west and to the Black Sea, the storied Danube and other tributaries to the east. In the early days of the "Grand Tour of Europe" one heard the phrase, "see Naples and die," and its harbor is certainly a delight. But one might also say, "see Istanbul and live," for there are few waterways in the world so varied, so permeated with beauty and history and with such potential for travel, commerce and commuting.

A part of my initiation into Turkey in the 1930's was a fabulous cruise on one of the small Bosphorous ferries which ply the length of that body of water. A friend, I thought, was teasing me when he said, "Now how would you like to have a tour of Europe and Asia for 50 cents?" Who would pass that one up! So, at Galata Bridge, separating the Bosphorous and the Golden Horn, we boarded the ferry and to my delight spent two hours shuttling between European Turkey and Asiatic Turkey. My Turkish friend commented, "This is the poor man's Cooks Tour." Years later, when my knowledge of Turkish had improved, I was asked one day to serve as interpreter for the famous photographer David Douglas Duncan. Remembering my early initiation, I suggested that we take the same trip to the Black Sea and back. He was an appreciative and fascinated voyager. The boatmen and passengers, mostly Turks, all wished to have their pictures taken and at every pier, both in Asia and Europe, there were invitations for coffee, offers of fresh swordfish, roasted chestnuts and even wine. Our progress was slowed down, but no one seemed to care. One of the most fascinating things about the ferries is the dexterity with which the boatmen, with huge ropes, snag the posts on the small piers with seldom a miss. In fact, they vie with each other to see who can wait the longest to make the pitch. For nearly six years I used to commute back and forth to the Galata Bridge from Bebek to my work at the Amerikan Dershane, YMCA in the old city. It was never boring. Friends who envied me called it my history major!

Lifted from one of my letters to my wife back in the USA is a Turkish tale about one day on the Bosphorous, and especially about the versatility of the harbor (I travelled in a motorboat):

4:30 A.M. At the Galata Bridge. Surprised the garbage men in their unpleasant task of loading the city trash. Followed them out into the Marmara where the city's garbage was dumped in deep water.

5:00 A.M. Back to the Galata Bridge to watch and welcome the ubiquitous fishermen coming to market with their catch from Black Sea, Marmara and Bosphorous.

7:00 A.M. Five Bosphorous Ferries converge from Asia, the Marmara and the Black Sea to unload the first commuters. "It is a miracle of Allah," observed a grizzled and tanned boatman, "that we seldom run into each other."

8:00 A.M. A great liner, filled with curious tourists steams gracefully into the harbor, looking like a great Castle of the Sea as it rounds Saray Point and anchors in the Bosphorous.

8:30 A.M. Several high-sterned fishing sloops, brightly-colored and high-masted, sail serenly into the docks as if they belonged. A Turkish boatman says with some scorn, "What do those Rums (Greeks) have to boast about? They are only sponge-fishermen, while we are the ones who put caviar and rare fish on the best tables in the world."

10:00 A.M. Now there is great excitement at the Galata Bridge for it is rumored that the President's yacht is sailing down from Anadolu Hissar (Anatolian Castle) with Ataturk on board. People around our boat are telling us to stay where we are and see the show, never a mention that foreigners should not get too near the Gazi (Ataturk). Their pride shows in their faces as the yacht slows down for the people to see Ataturk on the bridge. Today there will be a surprise at the yacht's destination in the Marmara for the President, anxious to be a man of the people, discarding all of the expensive trappings of the Sultans, is going to return the yacht to the people to use as they see fit. A rather cynical foreigner remarked to me afterwards, "It was a white elephant; why it costs $5,000 to start the darn thing." But it was a sincere gesture on Ataturk's part and the people loved it.

4:00 P.M. The rush-hour begins and watching this madness at the Galata Bridge, one wonders how anyone ever gets on the right boat. But they usually do and the mess untangles as the several ferry boats sail away again to Asia, to the Islands in the Marmara and up toward the Black Sea, a magic journey through history for some, for others just a routine return home after a busy day.

5:00 P.M. We are just in time to meet a group gathered at one of the piers on the European side for the evening excursion to the mouth of the Black Sea with picnic on board and return on the turbulent waters by moonlight on the shuttle route, back and forth, Europe to Asia.

In wartime or time of political unrest, however, boating is no longer just for pleasure, or commerce or commuting. It has its grimmer side. During my journey by boat around Africa in 1942, it seemed that no experience could be quite so frightening as running alone at night in the dark in strange waters without benefit of convoy. However, at the mouth of the Black Sea we later saw the "boat-people" grounded on an ancient freighter which had brought them through the Black Sea from Odessa. As if they had not suffered enough in the camps of Europe and in the hunger and cold of strange lands in between, these whole families of Jewish refugees, people without a country, were stranded again and caught in the middle of a war they had no part in. Since Turkey was neutral then there was no way it could give official help, nor could the Allies offer asylum, food, medicine and comfort. Their only hope was that some other country would take them in, because it was winter and anyone could see that this ship's arrival in Israel was very doubtful. Sadly, all passengers were later lost in a storm at sea.

Meanwhile, the International Red Cross working through some unofficial Turks saw that food, drinking water, clothing and fuel were taken to the ship. In an informal way also, some of the voluntary agencies cooperated in what we called Operation Desperation. We have always been glad for the little that could be done for these hapless people and when some of us passed their stranded vessel they would recognize us and wave. In the midst of man's inhumanity to man there is also man's impulse to be human and compassionate.

Another bleak experience with boats during the war involved American prisoners being returned via Russia on some old freighters. Our veranda on an old Turkish house where we lived was so near that we could communicate with people on board, and later, this time with Turkish cooperation, we were able to go on board with assistance. Miss Clary of the Girls Dershane and we at the Mens Dershane worked together to take clothing, food, gifts, reading matter (including Bibles) and just plain concern out to the people on board. The saddest were the mental victims, one of whom yelled every five minutes, and the children born in the war prisoner camps in Germany for whom the Girls Dershane needed to find diapers. The Turkish officials and people gave good assistance in this project. In some cases German women bribed the guards to let them visit American war prisoners. Their children lived with the mothers under frightful conditions in the women's prisons. Now on the way to America their stories were incredible recitals of bribery, brutality and despair. The compassion and aid of the Girls Dershane was most helpful.

Rumeli Hissar (the Roman Sentinel or old fort) on the
Bosphorous. Built in 1452
by Mohammed the Conqueror.

PROFILES OF YOUTH

"The Youth must surpass their leaders, and the children their parents."
Arab Proverb

How often have we heard serious parents in our country say, "I want my children to be better than I am." Perhaps this is a desire of parents everywhere. Certainly, in the Middle East every effort is made to give young people a good education and an opportunity for self-development. I asked one Muslim parent why it was that his family preferred to send their children to American schools. He replied, "Technically our schools are fine, but character-training is something we are just beginning to understand and value. I am not certain that I completely agree with his statement, for there are many good influences in the Muslim home and religion and there are dedicated teachers in their schools.

In the following profiles of young people I am not using real names out of consideration for their privacy:

AHMET. I met this young Arab Christian YMCA secretary at the request of an Arab staff member in the Jordan YMCA. He was then on the staff of the YMCA on the Israeli side of Jerusalem for the YMCA works on both sides of the line. The time was before the occupation of the West Bank by the Israelis, so we met in "no-man's land" near the Mandelbaum Gate. While there were guards at both frontiers, I noticed that they respectfully withdrew as we spoke. The secretary had come to inquire how he might obtain further education in an American university to equip himself for "Y" work. After an hour's interview I learned two things: one, that the young Arab, an Israeli citizen, was one of the most popular secretaries on the Israeli side, and two, that the reason why no one listened to our interview was because both the Arabs and Israelis trusted the YMCA, even in those tense times. Labib Nasir, Director of the YMCA in Jerusalem, Jordan, and former member of Staff in Jerusalem YMCA before the partition, deserves much credit for the respect and trust toward the "Y" on both sides in Jerusalem.

SELMA is a well-educated girl of prominent family in Tripoli, Lebanon. After college, which included business training she was offered several jobs by an oil firm and public schools but turned them down when she met some students in the language and commercial school under the Tripoli YMCA. The "Y" was able to give her considerably less but she felt the challenge to serve youth who were only slightly younger than she. With her competence and loving leadership, the school became recognized and its students favored for jobs in the business community. Also our International Committee in New York and the World's Alliance of YMCA's in Geneva provided funds to assist local funds raised in Tripoli to support the school. David Karam, chairman of the Local YMCA, as well as the National Alliance of YMCA's, encouraged the project which became co-educational.

IBRAHIM had been born and raised in a village in eastern Turkey where there had been a number of severe earthquakes. As a boy he went to public school, and there he became deeply attached to one of his teachers. This teacher was a good influence throughout the school and community. One day when the school was in session the most severe earthquake struck without warning, but as a beam fell from the ceiling and most of the students panicked, the teacher suddenly threw his body between the beam and the boy, saving the boy's life but losing his own. Even though he was only nine at the time, the incident haunted him and being a very thoughtful boy, he decided that he had been saved for some good life purpose.

Eventually, being poor but ambitious, he hitchhiked to Istanbul in search of further education and a skill with which he could make a living until he decided what he would do to realize the teacher's dream for him. Eventually someone recommended the YMCA School of Languages and Commerce to him, and the next day one of our staff said, "There is a very tired, thin little boy out there who insists on seeing you." The first thing we did was feed him, then we listened to his story. That was the beginning of a long association with a very bright and charismatic young man of 12.

Right in the middle of our talk with him another visitor announced that he must see us right away about entering his college nephew in the dormitory. While my Turkish associate dealt with him in a very tactful way, offering him coffee and reasons why he must wait, the lad and I were having Coca Cola in my office and were discussing his future.

Suddenly there was a frantic knock on the door and one of our staff said, "The gentleman says that if you knew who he was you would see him immediately," whereupon I went right out to see him. Here was this unprepossessing little man sitting on the edge of our second-best chair. He quietly informed me that he was the brother of Ismet Pasha, the President of Turkey, and that they wanted to place the President's son in our dormitory. I thanked him for coming, invited him to my office and offered him coffee. Then we signed his nephew up for the next vacancy in the dormitory just as we would anybody else, whereupon our little coffee man whispered in halting English, "But Mr. Yank, this is the brother of the President. Can't you give him better treatment? Allah kadir (Almighty God)."

Smiling for the first time, the President's brother said, "I like a man who is practical and forthright and who doesn't waste time giving extra compliments. Anyway, I heard about the boy who was visiting with you, and I want to meet him. He must be very special to take precedence over the brother of the President." There was no time to explain to the gentleman that we believed in equal treatment, insofar as possible, for all persons.

The boy called my wife his "mother" because she invited him to recuperate in our home from a tonsilectomy. He and our children became pals, learning English and Turkish from each other. Today he has a prominent position with the Socony Company. It all started with an earthquake in the ground, and in a boy.

HATICE, an Arab Muslim girl of prominent family, formerly of Palestine, worked as a nurse's assistant in a frontier town clinic. The frontier towns were those where the United Nations drew a rather arbitrary line between Jordan and Israel. Sometimes the line would divide a farm in two, so the Israelis had the farm and the Arabs the farm-house. The result was that neither one could make a living. The conditions in this frontier refugee camp were deplorable. A Canadian mission had come in and established a medical clinic which was doing a remarkable service. The United Nations was providing food, schools, some clothing, and Church World Service through the Near East Christian Council was providing help for farmers for the cleaning of ancient cisterns, for small loans that refugees might open shops and start business and for materials for weaving and other crafts through which refugees might make some pin money.

In the midst of it all was this smiling and competent Arab girl, a college graduate with sleeves rolled up, emptying bedpans, talking to frightened mothers about their babies and doing all kinds of small services. An American nurse with us on this visit said to the girl, "Your family must be wealthy; couldn't you be with them in Beirut and further your education and career instead of this?" "Yes I could, but then where would there be a challenge to compare with this?" was the simple reply.

Our four young people may never make the headlines or even receive the recognition they deserve, but it is from among such as they and their leaders that a brighter, more peaceful, Middle East will emerge. From what we know of Israel and what is happening among the youth there, they also are striving for peace. What would happen if they could by-pass the politicians and get together? Selam and Shalom are similar in meaning and they sound so much alike perhaps a bridge can be built between the deep differences and they can both learn to say "Peace!"

STRANGE FOODS AND FRIENDLY PEOPLE

There are all kinds of strange and wonderful names for favorite foods in the Middle East. Foods are deeply imbedded in customs and tradition. One of our favorites is "Imam Bayildi" (The fainting priest). Briefly, it is a stuffed eggplant filled with rice, chunks of meat, olive oil garnished with parsley and wrapped about with green and red chili. The black outer skin represents the priest's robes, the green chili his blouse denoting priesthood, the white headdress with its red band indicating that he has been a "Hadj" (pilgrim) to Mecca. The reason it is called "fainting priest" is because the priest is alleged to have fainted at its cost. It is a favorite dish for honored guests. It is also a fascinating conversation piece.

Some foods are somewhat difficult for foreigners to like but once you become accustomed to them they are even enjoyed. Among these one can list uncooked meat, smothered in onions garlic and herbs; the onions and garlic make one forget that the meat is uncooked. My most devastating experience with the unusual food was on a train where a middle class Turkish family watched me close my eyes and devour two bites near the eyes from a baked sheep's head. This is a real delicacy and rather delicious, if you can ignore the stare from the sheep!

In the Middle East a meal is not just a routine happening but a ceremony. In peacetime, at least, the meal is never hurried and even in the poorest homes your host will do without other necessities to share their best. In a modest home where one of our English students lived, the young man said to me with the honesty of youth after the dinner, "I am sure glad we did not eat everything, because my mother will cover this with cloth and it will be our diet for several days."

There are very interesting customs built around mealtime. My first experience at a formal dinner in a Turkish home was a near disaster. By tradition, the Middle Easterner is usually very quiet during a meal. However, at this meal the unexpected happened; guests at the table started to belch and it was all the more startling in the silence. Whoever briefed me on social behavior had not warned me that one must belch in order to show approval of the food. The lady next to me, who was an accomplished belcher, gave me a nudge and whispered, "Can you belch? It is their custom." In due time one becomes a belcher too, and does it with the best of them. There is also a custom which dictates that one cannot harm another person while the stranger is breaking bread with him, or her.

Dr. Shepard, a mission doctor, from Aintab, Turkey, used to travel horseback to remote villages where he conducted clinics for the sick. In those days one had to be alert for bandits and it was easy to "fall among thieves." The Doctor, familiar with the customs, always carried flat bread, cheese and olives in his gear.

One day, while traversing a wild and deep canyon his horse reared in fright and so he proceeded with caution. Around the next bend he came upon some men crouched in a circle eating out of a common dish in which they dipped their bread fork fashion. The Doctor acted quickly. Urging his horse toward the group and taking some bread in hand he bent over the large dish and scooped up some of the stew, got down from his horse and waited for an invitation. It was prompt and hearty.

He then recognized that their leader was a notorious bandit. After they had eaten and exchanged compliments, the Doctor said to the bandit, "Efendi, thank you for your hospitality but if you will excuse me I am a Doctor who has patients waiting for him in the village clinic." The Doctor, of course, was not certain that the host would continue to be friendly when they stopped eating so he dipped his bread again and waited. "May Allah give you protection," observed the bandit. "You know, Doctor Efendi, there are some wicked bandits around here so for your security I am sending two of my horsemen to accompany you to the village." Who knows what might have happened had Dr. Shepard not known the strange custom of "breaking bread in peace"?

Shepherds wear voluminous trousers with large pockets in which they keep their money, their bread, olives and cheese (favorites in their diet) and knives to ward off animals threatening the flock. The shepherds are also ready to share their meager fare with any stranger. This sharing of food, be it from a rich man's table, or from a poor shepherd in the fields, is a custom which is very good for food distribution. One friend used to call it "democracy of the stomach." In fact a biblical scholar has suggested that when the 5,000 were fed with the young lad's loaves and fishes, the people in the multitude, following their ancient custom, reached into their own supply of food and shared, which was another miracle to help the first one wrought by Jesus.

There is a saying in Arabic, "To feed your enemy is the next best thing to forgiving him." It is easy to understand, then, that there are very few people in that part of the world who starve. If there is scarcity, sharing helps fill the need. One of the customs during religious festivals is that the poor are fed first.

A lesson we learned about customs in the home was that often when you invite friends they bring an extra three or four along without asking. Two who showed up in this fashion are still our friends today. If your table is a plentiful one, then the servants let it be known in the neighborhood that the "Ev kadin" (housekeeper) is an excellent cook. One afternoon I came home early from work and found more people eating in the kitchen than we had invited for dinner. Just accept the fact that this is the custom and that a buffet meal is the answer to your problems.

Each year in Adana, Turkey, where I was stationed, the "Vali" (Governor) of the Cilician Province gave a feast for the American community at Government House in honor of Dr. Cyril Haas who had saved his wife's life through surgery. Food was the medium used for the Governor to express his gratitude to the Doctor. I remember counting the plates piled in front of me. There were thirteen of them. In my inexperience I remarked to the friend next to me, "Why do they have so many plates?" "They are for the thirteen courses we shall eat; since it is your first feast, you had better go easy on each plate." It was small comfort and sound advice.

Today, with food scarcities and inflation, I would like to believe that these charming customs continue and I trust they do. Certainly the Prophet Mohammed was wise when he taught the faithful to feed the poor first, and then feed themselves.

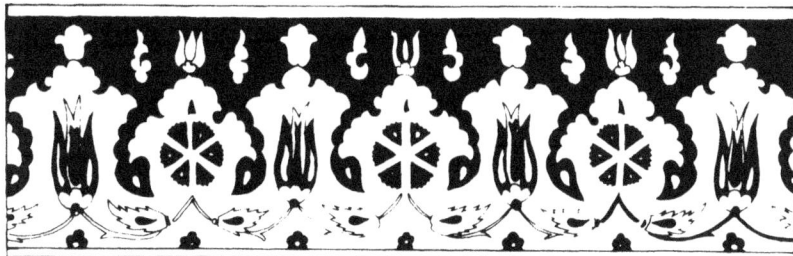

BLACK SEA VOYAGE
Istanbul to Soviet Frontier

It was at the end of the Second World War and our first holiday together in the Middle East. Perhaps it was risky to venture too far in any direction, but we decided to take the Black Sea voyage on a combined passenger-freighter of the Turkish Seaways. We could not have had a more peaceful or pleasant trip. Of course, the ship called only at Turkish ports on the southern shore of the Black Sea as far as Coruh.

My wife, Jessamine, and I learned later that Turkish friends had prompted their contacts in all of the ports enroute to look after our welfare. Because this was a combined business-pleasure trip, we were more official than we thought. The Turkish Kizilay (Red Crescent Youth Division) were co-sponsoring our trip and had asked me, as advisor to their summer camping program, to visit and evaluate their newly formed summer camps and youth recreation centers.

Moreover, we had been invited by a military commander and his wife to be their guests in Samsun on our return voyage. The General was the commander in charge of a vital part of the Black Sea coast and later in charge of Army personnel in Ankara. In the latter post he was in close contact with the American military aid program and its staff. He was greatly respected and liked by all who knew him. When we told our friends about the Black Sea journey and its purpose, they were envious of us.

Virtually unspoiled and untouched is the South Coast of the Black Sea, stretching for over 700 miles from Istanbul to the Soviet frontier. The combination of historic and colorful harbors, the vineyards, fruit trees and famous tobacco farms in the foothills of the coastal ranges, the deep blue, not black, sea, and the wide and pristine beaches, all formed a symphony of beauty which made our voyage a constant delight. Strange that here between a sometimes stormy and cold Black Sea and the snow-covered coastal mountains, there should be an almost tropical climate.

Due to our sponsorship by the Turkish Red Crescent Society, we were well-entertained on board ship and in the ports of Sinop, Trebizond and Samsun where we stopped over for a day or two of sightseeing and visiting youth centers. For entertainment on ship we had the best floor, or deck show one could want, for enroute to a folk festival in eastern Turkey were a number of very colorful folk dancers. One evening we shall always remember, they performed their local dances, including the Zaybek or handkerchief dance, for men only. The spectacle of a circle of men, each waving a small handkerchief, dancing to the drums, lutes and other instruments in the moonlight, was memorable. The beat is hypnotic.

At the Captain's table we heard stories of the seas around us from the Captain and first mate. There were toasts to everything and everyone, including the Americans, for we were in rather high favor at that time. It was so close to the war that the stories about it were very fresh and real to the hearers. There seemed to be an agreement that there might be a third world war soon.

It was on this adventure that I learned to play Tric-Trac (backgammon) while Jessamine got acquainted with the women who were unusually modern in dress and in their outlook.

After getting close enough to Soviet Russia so we could say we had seen it, and exploring the coast around Coruh and its fragrant tea plantations, we turned westward again, landing a few days later at Samsun, the end of the sea voyage for us. Samsun was really the high point of our voyage for there we experienced the warm hospitality of the General and his wife. Because of their keen interest in the youth, their home was filled with visitors nearly all the time we were there. The General arranged for visits to the local Red Crescent and Youth Centers. There was an openness and sincerity about the entire visit. I remembered again what an anonymous writer once said about youth, "There is healing and joy in being with them," and it was certainly true in Samsun.

One evening a slightly off-key military band entertained with a repertoire of jazz and semi-classical Turkish music. The leader of the band was Greek and the band itself was made up of Turkish, Italian and American youth. It was a delightful evening that gave the opportunity for both of us to try our Turkish, but more than that to make new friends with some of whom there is still correspondence. It was a joy to see Jessamine share her warm and sensitive friendliness with new acquaintances in this grass-roots setting. The entire trip that summer constitutes one of our finest memories, I presume because it was like going back in time to when life was more simple and trust and affection were the rule, rather than mistrust and hostility.

The day after the party we were loaded down with gifts of fruit for our train journey and with quite a delegation, including many young people we had met, wishing us a "bon voyage." Ahead of us was a most beautiful trip by train, first through the coastal range and then across the great plain to "Kayseri" (ancient Caeseria) where we had a week of rest and sightseeing at our Boys' Lycee at Talas before entraining for Istanbul where there was an equally friendly welcome. With some amusement I remember a rather sophisticated Turkish friend in Ankara saying to us before our trip, "What is there to see or do east of Ankara? It is just a bore." It was not the first time in our travels to hear someone speak with disparagement of parts of his or her country. On return through Ankara we stopped to see friends briefly and I can still see the amazement on the face of our critic when we remarked, "You ought to go east and see what you missed."

ISTANBUL
City of Charm and Contrasts

A noted historian once said of Istanbul, "It is a city almost inexhaustible in its interests and moods. I have come back again and again, but the fascination never ends." And even those who have lived most of their lives in this city on the Bosphorous experience the same fascination.

For one thing, it is almost unique among great cities of the world in that its history is horizontal. As one American archaeologist put it, very little digging is necessary to study the various levels of history in this city. In fact, if one goes on an historical tour of the city, as we did with a famed Turkish archaeologist, the main evidence of a dig of any proportions is in Sultanahmet, the "Old City" where the great Hippodrome was uncovered. Very little digging was necessary to explore the extensive cisterns of Byzantine times built in the fifth and sixth centuries under Aya Sofia (Sancta Sophia).

For ten years I had the privilege of working across the street from Aya Sophia where from my office at the Dershane I could gaze on this great Church-Mosque-Museum, and where I sometimes had coffee or lunch with Ali Sami Boyar, a Turkish painter and curator of the Museum. One never wearied of looking at the interior of this great edifice whose columns supported the largest dome in the world. On the outside were the equally amazing flying buttresses which, with the columns, carried the incredible weight of the dome. For most of the time while we were in the Middle East Professor Whittemore, an American authority on mosaics, worked with his staff to uncover the marvelous mosaics of the Christian era, a project encouraged and supported by Kemal Ataturk who, unlike other Turkish leaders in history, had a respect for foreign traditions and culture. It is sad to admit that the curator, M. Boyar and Professor Whittemore did not always agree, but both of them were experts in their fields and M. Boyar did his best to smooth over the differences. The professor was an eccentric and the artist-curator most sensitive and proud of the Islamic elements in the structure. One day when frustration on both sides reached the boiling point, M. Boyar sat in a chair beside the washroom painting while the professor hid inside to avoid a particularly obnoxious visitor. Someone has rightly said "one must look at the art apart from the artist." and when one does it is easy to overlook temperament and faults.

At the other end of the Hippodrome from Aya Sophia is an equally magnificent structure built to rival Aya Sophia — the Mosque of Sultan Ahmet I. Between these two edifices of the Christian and Muslim eras is a lovely garden. The Mosque, originally built with six minarets later had added to it a seventh because the priests insisted that only in Mecca could there be a Mosque with six minarets. So keen was the Sultan to rival the Church of Saint Sophia that legend says that on Fridays he would don laborer's attire and join the workmen on the scaffolding. The Blue Mosque, as it was later called, was built between 1609 and 1616. Its builder, Mehmet Agha, an apprentice of the great architect, Mimar Sinan, was a member of the Corps of the Janissaries whose works had been so praised that he was sent to Mecca to repair the Kaaba, or sacred stone.

The Blue Mosque gets its name from the lovely handmade blue tiles covering the rear of the mosque. Most of the designs on the tile depict flowers especially the carnation which is often used as a symbol in Islamic art.

Between the Blue Mosque and the Roman Aqueduct to the west is the noted University of Istanbul, surrounded by the covered bazaar in the midst of which sprawls the Mosque of Suleyman the Magnificent, itself a magnificent mosque. Here, under ancient olive trees are the outdoor coffee houses where the university students meet to listen to classical music and jazz, and to discuss religion and philosophy with some of the broader-minded "Hojas" (priests) from the seminary nearby. Sometimes they would invite me to join them and with my more mature Turkish at that time, I would learn of the aspirations and dreams of the youth and of the respect they had for those men older and wiser than they. One of the Hojas, a young man who was very popular with the university students and I became friends and I learned much from him during our coffee-time together. Once, at his invitation I removed my shoes, washed my feet and forehead and donned a head covering to take part in the worship at Suleymanyie Mosque. I remained in the background, but near enough to sense the rapt attention given by the students to the youthful priest. It was most unusual to see young people taking part in the "namaz" (prayers) and worship in a Muslim Mosque. I felt most honored to be invited to visit the services that day.

It is a pity that history hangs a cloud over the Sultan Ahmet Mosque, which could not be blamed on Sultan Ahmet, but a successor, Mahmud the IInd, who issued a decree for the Mosque in 1826, abolishing the Janissaries. This pogrom against the Janissaries who were foreigners in the eyes of the leaders of that day, came about partly because of the tendency of the Janissaries to ignore the Sultans and partly because of jealousy among the leaders of the remarkable gifts of the Janissary corps, who were accomplished in warfare, the arts and organization. Under the Sultan's orders, 10,000 of the Janissaries perished on Sultan Ahmed Place. It was a dark day in the history of the Turkish Empire.

Much of the charm and history of the old city is caught up in the interminable covered bazaars which were, in part, a horse stable in Byzantine times. Here are miles and miles of twisting tunnels with small shops, coffee-houses, and even small mosques on either side of cobbled streets. On warm summer days one often sees the most modern of women in their western dress mingling with the shyer, more traditional Muslim women who, although unveiled as all Turkish women are today, still follow the old ways. There is a welcome coolness in these ancient tunnels which remind one of the life-style of a day when most Middle-Easterners were Bedouins, and when the bazaars were a place for trade and a place for the caravans to rest when on long journeys.

Across the Golden Horn on the Galata Bridge is the section called Galata where one takes the tram up to the hilltop where the modern city of Pera looks down on a teeming harbor between the Golden Horn and the Bosphorous. In a few miles one steps out of ancient history into modernity, but one is relieved to learn before long that there is a pride and a respect for the old city with its bazaars , storied walls and seven gates, its beautiful mosques and churches and even the Palace of the Sultans where so much intrigue, glory and even violence took place. One evidence of this respect for history is the great crowds of local people and pilgrims one sees at festival time around both Muslim and Christian edifices. Another is the delight of the more educated Turks with the knowledge and appreciation of visitors and sometime foreign residents in their country.

In recent years a great suspension bridge has been thrust across the Bosphorous linking Turkey in Europe with Turkey in Asia. Before the bridge was built the Bosphorous ferry boats were the only means of crossing this historic waterway. At the dedication ceremonies of the bridge the point was well taken that this was but another stage in the development of Turkey as an important crossroads between Europe and Aisa. However, the prediction is that the colorful and energetic little ferry boats will still ply the Bosphorous and join the Marmara Sea Islands with the mainland. On a visit to Istanbul and the Bosphorous Lord Byron wrote the following lines:

'Tis a grand sight off the Giant's Grave,
To watch the progress of those rolling seas
Between the Bosphorous, as they lash and lave
Europe and Asia.

To see the Bosphorous so many times, and in so many moods and seasons is a privilege beyond describing. In her book "Beauties of the Bosphorous," Miss Pardoe, an English author, wrote, toward the end of the nineteenth century (the date is not recorded in her work) her first impressions of Constantinople. Unfortunately, "Beauties of the Bosphorous," published by Virtue and Co., London, is out of print. The original pen and ink drawings in the book by W.H. Bartlett are superb. Miss Pardoe wrote:

The great charm of Constantinople (now Istanbul) to an European eye exists in the extreme novelty, which in itself is a spell; for not only the whole locality, but all its accessories, are unlike what the traveller has left behind him in the West, that every group is a study, and every incident a lesson; and he feels at once the necessity of flinging from him a thousand factitious wants and narrow conventional prejudices, and of looking calmly and dispassionately upon persons and scenes wholly dissimilar to those with which he had been previously acquainted.

There is no better way to travel through the beauty and history of the Bosphorous than by boat. At night, especially, there is a magic you may not experience anywhere else in the world. The ancient, unpainted "Konaks" (summer homes) and magnificent Palaces of the Sultans, the great towers of "Hissar" built by Muhammed the Conqueror to aid in the capture of the city, the former Robert College now a Turkish school with its spectacular view of Asia and up and down the Bosphorous, the singular beauty of mosques, all delight the spirit and stir the imagination.

JERUSALEM — CITY OF THREE FAITHS

What better time to write this chapter about Jerusalem than on Christmas Eve, 1978? What better place than the southwestern part of our own United States? For the luminarias light the way for the Christ-child to our homes in New Mexico; the mesas and mountains remind one of Judea and Samaria; the adobe villages of the Spanish and the adobe pueblos of the American Indians remind one of the mud villages and their beehive houses of the Middle East and out here in the southwestern lands, whether people are on the desert, in the town or on the ranches, the stars seem nearer and clearer, as they always do in the brilliant heavens over Bethlehem and Jerusalem.

On Christmas Eve, Jerusalem is alive with excitement as men and women and children of many nations make their pilgrimage to the Holy City. Differences are forgotten, old enmities for the moment melt away and a city that has, in recent years, seen so much sorrow is filled with anticipation and joy. Muslims, Jews and Christians within these ancient walls, enter into this joy for Jesus has been recognized by all three faiths as a great prophet whom they honor and revere.

Even at a time when this great walled city's gates were closed by strife and divisions, some of us who had travelled down from Beirut on the United Nations plane were privileged to be in Jerusalem on Christmas, and I remember joining a group of friends by the Mandelbaum Gate to welcome Christian pilgrims from Israel crossing through no-man's land for the journey to Bethlehem. For once the guards on both sides lowered their guns and one could hear the greetings in Hebrew, "shalom", and in Arabic, "selam", both similar and both meaning "peace", echoing among the historic walls across the barriers. "If only it could be like this always," a pilgrim said to a relative on the Jordan side as they embraced. It was incredible that on the night before we had heard gunfire at this same point whereas the next day, in the spirit of brotherhood, people were greeting each other with shalom and selam. There seemed to be an agreement between the parties that for this one day and night Jerusalem would be a "City of Peace."

In America we sometimes forget that Jerusalem is a Holy City to all three faiths — Jew, Christian and Muslim — and that it should always be so. To the Jews, who were there in Old Testament times when it was called Salem, it is a sacred and holy place; to the faithful Muslims it is the third most holy city after Mecca and Medina; and to the Christians it is also sacred and holy for it was here and in nearby Bethlehem, where He was born in a manger, that Jesus in whom so many hopes were gathered, became a Christian prophet and the long-awaited Messiah and teacher.

Roughly, the Jews were there in Old Testament times, the Christians 1978 years ago and the Muslims 1,300 years ago. As living proof of their citizenship in the Holy City are the synagogues, Mosques and Churches; but beyond and above these are the contributions they made to the culture, the religions and the customs of Jerusalem. In particular they were unique in that they all worshiped one God, and in the case of the Jews and the Muslims, their origins were Semitic. While each of the faiths have made enduring gifts to the city in customs, religion, architecture, learning and government, it is my own conviction that Jerusalem should be an international city. "Jerusalem should be a city of world-wide culture as well as of political and religious harmony," Paul Anderson observes. One cannot help but note that the Christians living in Jerusalem owe much to the peoples, the religious beliefs and practices, the arts and the human qualities of the Jews and Muslims just as the other two faiths have benefitted from the Christians.

Of the many Christian sects in Jerusalem, the Greek Orthodox and the Armenian Protestant have perhaps made the most consistent impact and contribution. Their churches, orphanages, hospitals, schools and general influence have added richly to the community. Attesting to their presence are a number of institutions, art centers and architectural structures. Equally influential are the Anglican churches whose witness and good works have made for respect for their churches and leadership. The fact that the Archbishopric is located in Jerusalem has been a boon to the spiritual life of the city. Dr. Paul Anderson, former YMCA executive, distinguished authority on orthodox history and leading Anglican layman, has provided materials for the above statement.

It has been my privilege to visit Jerusalem and Bethlehem many times since my first visit in 1931 on my way to Turkey. As I returned in 1942 I could feel a mood of waiting and a stillness in Jerusalem as if it were waiting for some unexpected event. On the surface it was its friendly, but inscrutable self, but underneath there was a smell of change and unease. But the city still has an aura of unity.

I had come into Jerusalem as a guest of the YMCA, and so I stayed in what has been called the most beautiful YMCA building in the world, my wonderful hosts being Alvah Miller and his wife. Alvah served with his wife for many fruitful years as Franternal Secretary of the Jerusalem YMCA under the auspices of the International Committee of the YMCA, New York. The first thing they did was to take me up into the Jesus Tower atop the YMCA where we had an incomparable view of the city. It was a very moving experience, shared by many during the years of change although it symbolized something that was unchanging. Alvah said, "You will be interested to know that our Jewish and Muslim members are just as interested in this Jesus Tower as are the Christians and, what is more, they often come together to admire and meditate, each in his own way."

Later we watched a lively game of basketball at the "Y". On the team were the youth of all three faiths. It is almost a miracle that, even during the most tense times in Jerusalem, there was scarcely a day when the doors were closed and the program not in progress. An Arab Muslim member said to me, "This is the place where I feel the freest and where I have learned what the word brotherhood really means." One wonders where the members on that team are today, and whether their memories of those early friendships are helping to build a bridge among differences as they were in 1942.

One Christmas Eve we joined the pilgrims as they walked from Bethlehem across the alleged shepherds field to a cave near the YMCA hostel. While the YMCA makes no claim to this as the original field of the shepherds, one gets the feeling that the mood and the view of Bethlehem across the hills make it seem authentic. Thousands of persons from many nations gather around the cave on Christmas Eve where they are served kebab folded in flat bread. They eat in silence beside shepherds' fires and later joining together in song and story and watching the star stand still above the stable where Jesus lay. How moving it is and how different one feels when one leaves that holy place! How inspiring it is that many others in the Holy Land and around the world are gathering in fields and churches and wherever they may choose to remember and worship the Babe of Bethlehem!

It moved me to hope and pray that someday Jerusalem would be a city where all men and women and children would be free, where it would be an international city with its gates open to all to live in peace again without divisions, without fear and without greed, "a city built on a hill" to give light to mankind everywhere.

As I left Jerusalem for Istanbul I remembered that, just as the Millers had entertained me on the Israeli side, Mr. and Mrs. Nasir had done so so many times in their home and at the YMCA in Jordan on the Arab side. Labib Nasir, former staff member in the YMCA at Jerusalem, had moved with his family across to Jordan and had initiated a YMCA on that side. He performed wonderful work with refugees in the famous YMCA Vocational school in a refugee camp at Jericho. The vision, dedication, common sense and energy of these two Arab Christians and their staffs added up to a remarkable work in Jerusalem and Jericho. Many of the young refugees trained in the practical vocational courses in carpentry, mechanics, woodwork (furniture making) and other crafts at Jericho became self-supporting in Jordan and other Arab countries in the Middle East. While much of the financing of these centers came from local sources, the World's YMCA in Geneva and the International Committee in New York shared in helping to finance the services and in providing advisors for the center. Church World Service, through existing voluntary agencies in the middle east and other parts of the world also supported and encouraged the work. Mr. Nasir and I served on the Near East Christian Council Committee for Refugee Work. Through the major help of UNRWA (United Nations Refugee Works Agency) and its excellent staff, we had assistance in furnishing services to the people in the refugee camps.

THE UPROOTED

It may not be widely known, but from the times of the Spanish Inquisition (1237-1834) almost to the present, Istanbul has been a city with a large minority of refugees. Best known in chronological order have been: Spanish Jews, White Russians and those who fled from Germany during the Second World War. Perhaps the largest number came from Spain. In Istanbul one finds synagogues, schools and cultural institutions established by the Spanish Jews and others of Jewish origins. In general they were welcomed by the Muslim population, mixing well, prospering and learning the language . Their many gifts and skills have been appreciated. At one time, two of our staff and many of our students in the Dershane at Istanbul were Jewish.

Among the White Russian refugees there have been a number of former aristocrats, diplomats of Czarist Russia and fewer of the working class. Hence, when they fled to Istanbul, most were advanced in years. Among them were a few Poles, Lithuanians, Croats, Rumanians, Bulgarians and Yugoslavs, all having become refugees under the Communist regimes in Eastern Europe.

One case, of an aristocratic and courtly Polish diplomat was particularly touching. With the take over of the Polish Embassy by the Communists he lost his position and most of his belongings overnight. With great dignity he appealed to our committee (The International Rescue Committee) to have us print 200 calling cards indicating that he had represented Poland as a senior diplomat in Ankara. When we honored his request he said, "Merci beaucoup, for this is more important to me now than bread." After a visit in his cramped quarters, a hallway in a cheap hotel, one of the IRC members invited the Polish friend to his home as a guest.

On our International Rescue Committee we invited some refugees who had become self-supporting to serve. In one large apartment on the Bosphorous there were so many refugees from Germany that the bulding was called Hitler Khan. The former mayor of Berlin, Herr Ritter, was for a time the chairman of the committee. Both men and women served as advisors. Mr. Luther Fowle of the American Board Mission was a valued member. Herr Ritter used to say, "There are so many on our committee from the faculty of Istanbul University, that if we met during classes they might have to close the University."A Turkish professor observed, "We must thank Herr Hitler for sending us so many distinguished scholars." Just to name a few: a leading and world-renowned chemist; a leading and world-famed cancer researcher; the former finance secretary of the short-lived Weimar Republic; and a noted botanist. Not only in Istanbul, but at Ankara University, there were German refugee professors. Both students and faculty benefitted from the knowledge and presence of these "uprooted" scholars. They were well paid, respected and liked by the people for they quickly fitted into the culture and society.

With grants from the United States government and some local sources, a fund was established for the teaching of languages and commerce to young refugees who had escaped from Eastern Europe. The Girls and Mens Dershanes both received funds from these sources and established classes for the refugees. As soon as these youths became skilled, they were assigned to other countries for permanent citizenship. A few outstanding students went on to do graduate work at the universities or at Robert College. They were industrious, perhaps because they realized that this was their only chance for survival and acceptance. Someone suggested that we have separate classes for the refugees, but we thought it better to integrate them with other students and it worked well.

I remember one evening when a member of the staff came and told us that two of our refugee students were so dirty that their teacher had hesitated to let them in. When we talked with the refugees they said quietly, "The reason we are in this condition is because we parachuted into our country, stayed two weeks gathering information needed by the West. We just got back tonight, and did not wish to miss a single class. Excuse us for we have not bathed since we left."

Another unforgettable experience occurred at the Bulgarian border where we had gone to receive some 30 refugees originally from Russia who had been shunted around Europe for several years, and were now entering Turkey legally on visitors' visas. We confirmed the story they told about having been placed in the wrong car (for freight) to be shipped by rail to Sofia, Bulgaria, instead of Western Europe where they were told they would be going. Their welcome in Bulgaria was not a warm one officially, but they did tell us how some of the Bulgars at great risk helped them. I had been asked to go along on the mission because of my knowledge of Turkish. Miss Jane of the World Council of Churches, Geneva was the competent leader of the team; we also had with us a Yugoslav refugee with a working knowledge of several European languages as well as English. With us from the Dershane was B..., a fine young teacher and a Fulbright Scholar who was serving in the "Y". We had two cars, one from the American Consulate and our Jeepster. Little did we realize when we drove into Adrianople, the town near the Bulgarian border, that bureaucracy would keep us waiting for two days before our refugees could enter Turkey. The delay was due to triangular phone calls involving Geneva, Sofia and Adrianople, with most of the holdup in Sofia. Time was lost also in communicating the long Russian names of thirty people in three different languages over an antiquated telephone system.

Once the delays at higher levels were over we found the border officials on both sides accomodating. In the Turkish customs office particularly, there was cooperation and hospitality. We did not count the gallons of coffee and tea consumed nor how many shish kebabs we ate!

Finally, the second evening, in a pouring rain an ancient bus pulled up to the Bulgarian border and our charges disappeared into a building from which they emerged two hours later. We could imagine how weary and hungry they were after a long drive from Sofia. From Istanbul the Ladies Auxiliary of the Girls Dershane had thoughtfully sent packages of fruit and sandwiches for the refugees and this was the first thing we gave them when they crossed over into Turkey. The stories they told us were incredible. Our Fulbright student observed through his tears, "No novel could ever equal their story."

As we left the Turkish customs after less than an hour, an elderly Russian refugee embraced one of the young customs men and said with tears in her eyes, "I shall always remember you in my prayers!" What we did not tell our refugees was that the Turks were eager to do almost anything to get even with the Bulgars! Later that night in Adrianople the townspeople turned out to have a feast for the refugees, one of whom went around the table afterwards picking up left-overs because she could not believe there would ever be that much food again. It was a day that will live in my memory forever.

Part of the ruins at Silefkiye,
an ancient Greco-Roman city near Tarsus.
(Photo by Clark-Adana.)

THE ALMOST IMPOSSIBLE MISSION

In 1957, during very sensitive times in the Middle East, we were asked by the International Committee of the YMCA to serve in Lebanon. Everyone thought that the invitation had been initiated by the National Movement in Lebanon, but on arrival in Beirut, it seemed that the initiative was almost entirely with the local YMCA. Not that it mattered that much; we were wanted and that did matter.

Moreover, when we thought all hurdles had been surmounted, the word came back to New York that there was still one more. We were asked if we would be willing to use only the first letter in my given name and to be known as Mr. and Mrs. E. Porter Young (since my first name, Ezra, was Jewish)? My wonderful and wise mother remarked sadly, "I never thought my son would sell his birthright for a mess in the Middle East." She was more prophetic than she realized. As a matter of fact, shortly after arrival we discovered that nearly everyone knew my first name anyway. That included the police, and the name seemed to make little difference.

Since the call to Lebanon included the urgent message that we were needed "as of yesterday" we made plans to take our children out of school in February, to go to New York for final arrangements and sail on the Queen Mary for Europe all in a few weeks. My wife, who was a meticulous packer, indicated to the movers in Harrisburg where we had been stationed, that there were four piles of books and that they were plainly marked. The first pile, the most important, was labeled "take with"; the second "sell"; the third "give away"; and the fourth "leave in storage." Somehow, in the excitement of moving "take with" got shunted into "store" and we did not discover the mistake until we unpacked in Beirut.

After a few days in London as guests of the first YMCA ever founded we went on to Geneva to be the guests of Paul and Anna Limbert. Paul was then General Secretary of the World's Alliance of YMCA's We could not have had finer hosts or better sponsors on our way back to the Middle East. As we got nearer Beirut it seemed the more we learned about the situation the more eager we were to reach our destination. One former leading figure in the Egyptian government, now in exile in Europe whom we met through Dr. Limbert, was very helpful in several briefings. At our last session he said, "If I were in your shoes, considering all of the tensions and problems out there, I believe I would be tempted to go back home on the next boat." Anyway, his other advice was excellent.

Since we were going to the Middle East where there were over 1,000,000 Palestinian refugees, the staff in Geneva thought it would be well for us to visit Austrian refugee camps where there had been much experience with refugees during, and since World War II. Later, as the YMCA dealt with refugees in the Middle East, we were glad to have had this background. Also, since my family was with me, it was an opportunity for all of us to share in the visitation to camps and do some sightseeing on the side. When a guide in Austria approached us and asked whether we were on a tour, Maja said, "Yes, we are on Daddy's tour." In fact, our children and our YMCA friends in Austria were the very best guides we could have had. At one border the police were so fascinated with our two young people that they almost forgot to ask for our passports.

On return to Geneva, we spent another few days in conferences with the World Alliance of YMCA's staff who, with the International Committee, were our co-advisors. In addition, the YMCA people in Geneva had set up visits to the headquarters of the World's YWCA, the World Council of Churches and the International Red Cross. These briefings we found very helpful during our years in Beirut. We left Geneva reluctantly but we did stay long enough to meet many fine people, some of whom are now lifetime friends.

From Geneva we crossed through the Alps by train to Venice. How lovely the mountains and the sea were in the spring. From romantic Venice we boarded a steamer, went through the fabulous Adriatic to Greece and the Mediterranean to beautiful Beirut. David was resting in a deck chair when a curious tourist inquired, "How do you like your trip?" David, always polite, said "This is not my first time, you know." The information and knowledge gained in Austria and Switzerland prepared us well for the stormy and challenging years in Beirut.

Mr. Ibrahim Chemayel, secretary of the Beirut YMCA, and his Chairman, Mr. George Ashkar, met us at the boat and took us through teeming Beirut to a hostel near the American University where we were to stay until we found a permanent home. We were grateful for the help of these two gentlemen. Here we acted like tourists for several weeks, awaiting developments. I had heard the warning many times, "Do not try to hurry the East." So we were resigned to waiting. However, when we aksed about the YMCAs in other parts of Lebanon and how one could visit them, we drew a blank. Soon we suspected that what we had heard enroute was true, that "the two different factions were at odds and not communicating" so that left us caught in between. Having been in the Middle East before, I decided to be patient and so we planned to go sightseeing in the mornings and swim afternoons. It was spring with the fragrance of vari-colored semi-tropical flowers; the sea was very blue and tempting and the beaches and mountains beckoned. Beirut, built on a promontory jutting into the sea with magnificent Mt. Lebanon as a backdrop, is in a country rightly called "the Switzerland of the Middle East." My son soon discovered that he could ski in the mountains above the Cedars of Lebanon in the morning and swim in the afternoon in the warm Mediterranean. The family was delighted while I was chafing at the bit to begin my job. One day when we were at the beach the children said, "Daddy, will you relax? You haven't spent so much time with us for months." That was the nudge I needed. But I spent several hours a day studying Arabic which I found ten times more difficult to learn than Turkish and I made a conscious effort to get in touch with the other YMCAs.

One morning I received two phone calls: one from the Tripoli YMCA in northern Lebanon resulting in a date with the secretary and chairman to come and visit us, and the other from the secretary of the local YMCA saying he needed my advice right away. I was delighted and said to my wife, "At last, after four weeks they need me." Hurrying to the local "Y" in the old city of Beirut, I found the secretary. "I have tried to reach you all morning," he said with some impatience. "You see, we are having a ping pong tournament tonight and I needed your advice about where to put the chairs." My disappointment and frustration were carefully hidden and I took great pains to place the chairs as I thought they should be. But to myself I thought, "For this we took our kids out of school, pulled up our roots in America and travelled 8,000 miles, just to advise somebody where to put the chairs.!" On second thought, however, I put myself in Mr. Chemayel's shoes and realized that this was important to him and that it was a device to use my services before someone else did. I understood later that one official said, "The American advisor has finally gone to work."

The session with the chairman and secretary of the Tripoli YMCA was very enlightening and hopeful. It began officially and ended with a measure of warmth and understanding. There began an acquaintance with Messrs. David Karam and George Sleiman which became a friendship and a working relationship that I have treasured through the years and which lead, after two years to the establishment of a shaky but nevertheless unified YMCA movement called the National Alliance of Lebanese YMCAs. At least both factions were able to meet together in the same room and the real challenge of the needs of the youth in Lebanon helped them forget their differences and forge a fellowship which brought them closer together.

This was an authentic breakthrough and from that time on there were an increasing number of requests, projects and challenges, so that I scarcely had time for family and other personal matters. During the next five years three new YMCAs were developed and the National Alliance came of age as an advisory group. The three new YMCAs were started in refugee camps where they were sorely needed for, except for the schools, there were no recreational or social activities to speak of. Later on the World's Alliance of YMCAs in cooperation with the Lebanese National Alliance provided personnel to plan a much-needed leadership training course to train young refugee leaders in recreational, social and counselling activities. This program also helped to unify the movement throughout the Middle East. Our National Alliance chairman, Mr. Karam and Professor Nabih Faris, head of the Arab Studies department at the American University in Beirut and a Palestinian, gave sacrificial leadership and counsel to this new project. Working with them on a refugee services committee were many others. It was, indeed, an indigenous project and one that everyone agreed was worthwhile. As the YMCA work in Lebanon grew in stature and in favor my wife remarked, "Your patience and discretion paid off." My son added his comment, "For once, Pop, you said very little!" May I add: the support of my wife, the children, the National Alliance of Lebanese YMCAs and YMCA friends in Geneva and New York have been a tower of encouragement and strength to me for all those years in Beirut.

We visited the Palestinian refugee camps frequently, marveling at the raw courage and ingenuity of the teachers, social workers, pastors (Mullahs, Muslim priests), doctors and nurses, as well as the UNRWA workers and volunteers. Without them and the help of concerned people in the West and Arab countries, the plight of the refugees could have been unspeakable. Still, the suffering of these uprooted people, often living in tents and often hungry, cold and unemployed was very real. Over all was the bitterness of their uprooting from their homes and farms in Palestine.

Elsewhere, in the chapter on "Anatomy of a Revolution," I write of how, during the 1958 troubles, the YMCA shifted gears to meet a crisis which destroyed many lives and some institutions but the "Y" never closed its doors to youth on either side of the conflict.

The street called "Straight" in Damascus, 1932.

THE OTTOMAN HERITAGE

If you were told that one of the greatest empires in history had been founded by the semi-legendary Ertoghrul, head of a nomadic tribe from Asia consisting of only 445 families, you might think it mere fantasy. "These nomads became the first people of mid-Asia to break their way into Europe, there to stay and rule," writes Harold Lamb in his book, "Sulieman the Magnificent." They were the pioneers who founded the Ottoman Empire which ruled for over 600 years.

The campaign of Ertoghrul and his forces is a story of "Kismet", a battle of honor and a gift of land in Asia Minor. While relatively small and infertile, this land became the beachhead of the new empire.

The battle which Ertoghrul watched from a high hill overlooking the plain was one between the Seljuk Turks, then in power but also showing signs of decline and the Mongols roving Asia Minor and devouring whom they knew to be weak. Ertoghrul, seasoned warrior and wise leader, could tell that the Seljuks were no match against the might and cunning of the Mongols, so he led his own men on horseback into a battle which resulted in the defeat and rout of the Mongols. Alaeddin, Sultan of the Seljuks, was so grateful to Ertoghrul for this last minute rescue that he took him to Konya, ancient Iconium, the Seljuk capital, where he was given every honor and the gift of land. Thus Ertoghrul — caught between two decaying empires, the Byzantine and Seljuk — and his son, Osman, were free and able to dream of and plan an empire going far beyond Turkey's borders. The men of the hour and history came together and for a time this changed the map of both Asia and Europe.

In Funk & Wagnals Dictionary, the Ottoman Empire is defined as follows:
A former Empire (1300-1919) of the Turks in Asia Minor, N.E. Africa, and S.E. Europe; Capital, Constantinople, also called the Turkish Empire.

Dr. Kingsley Birge, Missionary of the American Board of the Congregational Church in Turkey for many years and a Turkish scholar and authority on the Ottoman Empire, once said, "No one writing of the Middle East should overlook the lasting contributions of the Ottoman Turks." An earlier writer called the Osmanli Turks, "Magnificent Men with a Mission."

Beginning with Ertoghrul, the rough-hewn nomadic warrior seldom out of saddle, and ending with Suleiman, the Magnificent, somewhat shy, but sophisticated and an intellectual rather than a warrior, there were nine great Ottoman leaders, not one of them a weakling. Harold Lamb states, "It [the Empire] had been accomplished by no miracle or God-given fortune but by the ability of the Osmanlis themselves — by the exertions of nine extraordinary men. Osman had worn the coat of a rough animal hair. Selim had worn the banquet robe of spun gold."

Unfortunately, much has been written or said about the Ottomans which is negative and there is good reason for some of this negativism. However, one would think that any empire lasting as long as this one must have had leaders with the vision and ability to govern beyond the ordinary. Regardless of how worldly-wise they might have become along the way, they did not forget their nomadic beginnings in Ertoghrul and Osman nor were they corruptible except as some of their advisors in later years led them in corrupting ways. Actually, they started out with honor and with a certain desert Puritanism. They sometimes tried other means than military conquest to take over territory and power.

When young Mohammed the Conqueror at 27 years of age toppled the decaying Byzantine Empire in 1453, there was no punishment of those who obeyed the law. In fact, Mohammed called on the Orthodox Patriarch at his seat in Fener on the Golden Horn to assure him that he and his people would be unharmed and that they would have their religious freedom and civil rights respected. The wonder of it all was that later, even when some of the Sultans were despotic in their rule, this protection of the rights of foreigners and minorities was still honored. One cry of the Ottomans as they went into battle was, "In war merciless; in victory benevolent." When Suleiman's armies conquered parts of Europe, the people were astonished at the fair treatment they had after battle. This disarmed the defeated who expected the worst from "those barbarians frm the East."

One incident in the capture of Constantinople from the Byzantines is noteworthy. To surprise the city, Mohammed's warriors built barges up the Bosphorous and took them overland in the night on rollers. The Venetian and Genoese navies thought they saw a mirage when, at dawn, the amphibian fleet descended to the Golden Horn. It was a masterful maneuver and the navys withdrew in disarray. Byzantium became a birthday gift to the youth, Mohammed, and gave the nations under Islam a beachhead on Europe. For the Greeks, those admirable people who had nurtured great philosophers and laid the foundation for democracy, it was only a temporary setback and disaster, but also a lesson never to ignore the people of the East.

Even the Americans benefit from some of the heritages of the Ottoman Empire; certainly Europe, then living through the Middle Ages, benefitted not only from the great art and architecture in the Alhambra and the spread of knowledge and the arts of the East which came along with the conquests of southeastern Europe, but from a strange encounter with Asian nomads who somehow had learned the arts of organization and empire better than those whom they had defeated.

Again, Kingsley Birge, in his excellent work, "A Guide to Turkish Area Studies," writes of the Ottomans:

> The Turks were most certainly more civilized and less nomadic than has generally been supposed. There is evidence to show that Osman had at his command well-organized forces ("Ahi", a type of semi-religious, mercantile, and perhaps military society). But the Turkish advance seems to have taken the form of gradual infiltration more than outright conquest.

Selma Ekrem, the granddaughter of the great social poet, Namik Kemal, says in her fascinating work, "Turkey, Old and New,"

> The Ottoman Empire was also the center of culture, art and industry. While the Janissaries carried on the art of warfare, Turkish architects filled the cities with their masterpieces.

Mosques of unusual beauty, some adorned with tiles, were erected, fountains and palaces and libraries were built and endowed by the Sultans or by prominent and wealthy individuals. The famous Kutahya factories turned out tiles whose exquisite textures and colorings rivalled those of Iran . . . Our museums are filled with works of art of skilled craftsmanship, hand-written and illuminated books and Koran [Muslim Bible] which the artists of that time left as a legacy to the nation, rugs, pottery and brocades.

Perhaps it is not necessary to note that the Janissary Corps, a creation of the Turks, was a group not only practiced in the arts of war, but skilled also in government and other arts and who had been taken prisoner by the Ottoman Empire in various military campaigns. They were usually of Christian background. They were in strong favor with most of the Sultans and a few of them had influence beyond their station in the Palace. Until the latter years of the Ottoman Empire, when their power and influence caused jealousy in the palace, they were for the most part accepted and honored.

Again, I quote from Selma Ekrem's book, "Turkey, Old and New," as she speaks of the capitulations which finally led to the downfall of the Ottoman Empire:

. . .A system which weakened the Empire and one of the main causes of its downfall, was the Capitulations, or special privileges granted by the Sultans to the foreign powers. All foreigners in Turkey had their own laws and could not be tried in the Turkish courts. They did not pay taxes and all the goods imported into the country from abroad were exempt from customs duty. The Capitulations encouraged the European powers and the minorities to wring concessions which finally reduced Turkey to a mere colony of Europe.

As to religious freedom, education and cultural activities among the minorities, the Ottoman Empire was surprisingly advanced for its time. Mrs. Ekrem writes:

Although the empire was ruled by the Sultan who was also the "Caliph," or head of all the Muslims in the world, religious freedom was enjoyed by all the subjects even under the rule of absolute despots. The Christian and the Jewish minorities were not compelled to adopt the religion and culture of their conquerors and each distinct religious group was organized under their own religious leader and enjoyed a great many privileges. The minorities worshipped in their own churches and synagogues undisturbed at a time when bloody religious wars shook Europe and the Jews were persecuted throughout the world. . .The minorities had their own schools where the teachings of Turkish was not obligatory. . .thus these groups in the empire retained their own language, customs and clung to their identity. . . The Ottoman Empire was a unifying force and under it the Balkans and the Near East enjoyed a long period of peace and prosperity which they had not attained previously and unfortunately do not possess now.

One wonders what that part of the world would be like today if the

Ottoman Empire had not declined and decayed in its latter years. But there are parts of the heritage it left to the world that have survived and they are enough to stir our imagination and win our admiration.

An ancient irrigation wheel near Istanbul in 1944.

FOCUS ON THE FAMILY

After being in Turkey for a few weeks I learned how much the family means in that part of the world. Having a room in the Mission House of the old city of Adana, I soon came to know Dr. William Nute and his family, but it was some time before I fully appreciated their friendship and advice as I adjusted to a new country, new customs, new job, new language and a different environment. Mary and Bill Nute and their two children living with them were a delight and a constant source of comfort and help. Just as Miss Lillian Brauer, director of the social and playground work in which I was assigned, was of invaluable assistance in briefing me, so was the Nute family.

Cyril and Maryle Nute were pals almost from the start. They liked nothing better than to teach me Turkish. Maryle's language was not exactly classical; she had a charming way of mixing English and Turkish in which the servants encouraged her. One day she fell from her high chair and amused us all by saying, "Ben get down dum" (I got down!). Cy was more dignified and modest in his speech, but he knew the language well enough to play with the Turkish children in the neighborhood. One day in the midst of a drought afflicting the Cilician Plain and when his parents were away, I heard a clatter in the streets and a rather familiar voice saying over and over again, "Bodi, Bodi" (Behold!). Cy, stripped to the waist and holding a tree branch over his head, had joined the Bodi boys who march through the streets saying an incantation for rain. Cy was not just one of the gang, but the leader! When I told his mother, she said, "That means he is accepted, good for him." But one part of being a Bodi boy was to submit to a tin of water thrown over your head and Cy said, "I think they made me leader so I would get most of the water."

Cy used to tag along when I went to work in the boys' playground and the kids loved that, and I benefitted from Cy's rather mature advice. He was accepted and appreciated at the playground too and became known as my "Yar Direktor" (vice-director) and "Tercuman Efendi" (translator). Every now and then Cy and I would slip away to a grade B or C western movie which we enjoyed so much. One night the show was later than usual and when we arrived home it was quite dark. Cy would never admit that he was scared but I disregarded that until he went upstairs to the apartment where the Nutes lived, returned in a moment or two reporting, "It's allright Mr. Young, there are two lumps in the bed and one of them spoke to me."

One day Cy stopped going to the playground with me and we all missed him. His mother said, "Cy told me you don't need him anymore because you have learned Turkish." Maybe I did not need him as translator, but I told him I surely needed him as assistant director. The next time we saw Cyril he was a computer engineer on assignment at NASA in Houston and in our reminiscences he reminded me that he came to me in tears one day with his model airplane saying, "According to all the laws of the universe, this darn thing should fly, but it doesn't."

The courage, humor, patience and kindness of the Nutes made many friends for them in the Turkish community. Mrs. Nute and her first husband had been missionaries in Adana before and during the Turkish-Armenian troubles and by accident he had been killed in the streets. Mrs. Nute decided that she wanted to return to Turkey to give her witness and to her joy when she and her second husband William Nute were sent to Turkey they were assigned to the American Hospital in Adana. However, it was some months before Dr. Nute secured permission to practice medicine so during this time he studied Turkish, read up in his profession and taught in the girls Lycee in Adana. It was in this interim period that I was privileged to meet them and to be accepted as one of the family.

The second family I met in Adana was Turkish; Semih Temel, an architect, and his Hungarian wife, Elizabeth befriended me and patiently taught me the language, customs and history of Turkey. They were one of the most cultivated families I have ever known. When I returned to Turkey during the Second World War, I met the Temels again in Istanbul. We renewed our friendship and they invited me to live in the garden apartment of their old Turkish house on the Bosphorous until my wife could join me. Every Friday evening for two years, the Temels and their two daughters invited me for dinner and the evening with them. I believe that I was the envy of many in the American community because of the nearness to the Temels. When my wife, Jessmine, joined me, they became her friends, too, and loved her as everyone did. Semih said, when he heard we were looking for an apartment, "Our second floor is vacant, why don't you move?" So we moved in to a 300 year old wooden house on the Bosphorous with a giant living room, an ancient Turkish bath, a six-terraced garden, a charcoal oven, a well — in lieu of an ice box — and a Turkish maid whom we inherited and who practically ran our lives from then on. Jessamine said, "I shall never complain, because we are together, and we have the Temels for neighbors. Who needs an ice box, let alone a Frigidaire." so Jessamine never complained, but she was delighted when I brought home an antique ice box and an ice cream freezer, bought in the covered bazaar for $10.50. Semih and Elizabeth Temel called them our status symbols and, for once, we had the pleasure of inviting them for dinner.

When my wife first came to Turkey in 1944, we lived for a while in the home of Huntington Damon at Robert College where his father had been librarian. Hunt was director of the United States Information Service where Jessamine eventually became his secretary. What a great help Hunt was in our orientation. And it irked me that I was only able to beat him once in tennis! A few days before we moved into our new home with the Temels, I very proudly took Jessamine to our vast "castle" on the Bosphorous to show her the furniture I had rounded up as a surprise for her. When she saw the rather sad collection of old chairs and tables, rugs and plates, pots and pans, and pictures, she sat down in a shaky rocker and began to cry. I thought it was with joy, for manlike I had decided that I had done pretty well, considering it was wartime. Her tears stopped when I produced a beautiful Bukharra rug for a centerpiece in the livingroom. A few years later she told me that the tears had been genuine.

In spite of its limitations, that home on the Bosphorous was one of the happiest ones we ever knew. Its name in Turkish, "Yilanli Yali" (the snake house) may not have sounded very fetching, but legend says that once, when the Grand Vizier lived in the house, he brought the Sultan of the day up the

Bosphorous for a visit and the Sultan was ecstatic about the location and about the summer home. Having noted that the Sultan admired the home very much and having remembered that when one admires something one must present it to him — especially to a Sultan, the Grand Vizier also remembered that the Sultan feared and disliked snakes, so with a straight face the nervous Vizier said, "Thank you, your Excellency for admiring my Palace, but I must remind you that it is full of snakes." So far as we know no one ever saw a snake there, but there were a few rats who multiplied more rapidly than one could dispose of them. When we stopped disposing of them our Turkish maid was elated and said, "You know we believe in transmigration, and I just hated to see you kill even a rat that may have been my grandmother." After that we had a truce with the rats. So much excitement, and so much joy and fulfillment we had in our jobs, our home and in the midst of the beauties of the Bosphorous!

A beduin father and son in Aleppo, 1933.

FROM BEHIND THE VEIL

The place of women in the Middle East was emphasized to me during the first two weeks of my stay in Turkey. My Turkish teacher invited me to his home for dinner, but when I arrived only the menfolk in the family welcomed me, and only they sat at the table. I remembered Mehmet Bay telling me that his mother and sister would stay in the kitchen and I would not meet them until we were better acquainted. In conversation at dinner I sensed that the father was of the "old school," and not too happy over Ataturk's sweeping reforms, including the freeing of women from the veil and the discarding of the Fez. Mehmet Bay confided that his father sometimes still wore his Fez around home although it was "Yasak" (forbidden). During a delicious and ample meal I noticed that a curtain at one end of the room was swaying slightly and that there was a peekhole at eye level. Later, as we left the "Selamlik" (men's quarters), my teacher told me that his mother and sister could see me from the "Haremlik" (women's quarters) and that they even remarked about my appetite and how they approved of my appearance. One day before I left Turkey there was another dinner, and the father allowed the women to serve us and even to have conversation, but not to remove their veils. However, this was unusual even in the provincial town during the Republic and I understood that before many years the father changed his mind.

In spite of our means of communication and of up-to-date information on the media in this country, we have many myths about life in the East. One is that many of the women still wear veils and stay strictly at home; the other that the men still wear swords and look to their women for convenience and pleasure. Of course, there are male chauvinists everywhere, but it is no more healthy for them there in Muslim countries than it is today in the United States.

Our artist and friend, Ali Sami Boyar, whom you met previously in these pages, and his wife became close friends of ours. They travelled widely and one evening he told us an amusing story of an incident in London. Because they were interested in knowing the people instead of just staying in one of the large hotels, they decided to seek out a small neighborhood hostelry. While the other guests were curious about these foreigners, it took a few days for them to thaw out and then they began asking questions about where they were from and of what nationality. The British friends having guessed almost every place in Europe and the Orient except Turkey, the Boyars informed their fellow-guests that they were Turks! At that point, the men retired to their hideaway for "a spot of ale," and the women took Mrs. Boyar in tow toward the tea room. Before they separated, Mr. Boyar commented with considerable glee, "I see you have the Harem and the Selamlik, too." Over the ale, for the artist was not a strict non-alcohol drinking Muslim, the men asked their guest, "So, how many wives do you have?" Sensing some gossip, they drew closer to Boyar and he became very dramatic, saying, "You see I am a practical man, so I choose my English-speaking wife to come to your country;

my wife who knows Russian, when we go to Moscow; the one with the knowledge of Arabic when we visit Egypt; and the one who "parle Francais" when our destination is Paris." This seemed to satisfy their curiosity. Later they were told that Mrs. Boyar was a linguist, knowledgeable and fluent in all of the languages mentioned.

Another myth about women in the Middle East is that the restrictions on them are rooted in Islam. The seclusion of the women was a device used by rather untutored Hocas (Muslim priests) who invented this excuse to keep women in their place. During the Prophet Mohammed's lifetime the women were not secluded and there is nothing in the Koran nor in religious custom to restrict women. In fact, Mohammed had great regard for women. He once said, "Paradise lies beneath the feet of a mother."

Selma Ekrem, well-versed in the customs and history of her people, writes in her book, "Turkey, Old and New":

> There was a time when Turkish women were absolutely free. Reading the old books and documents dealing with the life of the Turks before the conquest of Istanbul (1453) one finds that women were considered the equal of men by our ancestors. They were neither veiled nor secluded and the family was under the joint guardianship of both parents. Widows were the sole guardians of their children and managed their own property and money. Even the queens of old were not mere showpieces and no edict could become valid unless it contained the signatures of both the King and his consort.
>
> How, then, did the Turkish women lose their ancient freedom? When the Turks conquered Byzantium they discovered veiled women and apartments where they were segregated because the Byzantine Greeks did not allow their women much liberty. The Turkish men were much impressed with what they saw and it began to dawn on our ancestors that it might not be such a bad thing to keep women at home. As our Sultans became more and more autocratic, women, too, were restricted and generally lost every right they had had for many centuries. . .This great event in Turkish history, the capture of Istanbul, marks the beginning of life behind the curtain and behind the veil. . . Imperial edicts were even issued to control women's dresses and their behavior. . .In 1807, officials were appointed to check up on the laws regulating the opening of a woman's dress. . .If the official caught a dressmaker with a gown having a lower neck than that prescribed by the edict, the dressmaker was immediately punished!"

The progress that women have made in the Muslim world over the past 50 years has been remarkable. In Turkey, which set the pace under Ataturk, it has been more rapid but the Arab women have not been far behind. Dr. Nejla Izzedin, a pioneer among Arab women and a neighbor of ours in Beirut, wrote "The Arab World", a scholarly and fascinating book (1953) in which she made the following historical observations about Arab women:

> Western people associate seclusion and the veil with Arab and Moslem women. It is seldom realized that side by side

with this institution there was a long and well-established tradition of liberty. The tradition goes back to the Arabian desert before the rise of Islam. In the desert women participated fully in the whole structure of society. There were no occupations to which she was limited and none from which she was excluded. She shared the hardships of desert life with her mate and like him developed the qualities of survival in its rugged environment. . .here there was no room for the idle; consequently society did not look upon the woman as an ornament or an object of luxury or pleasure. With the hardships that she bore she carried the rewards and satisfactions of freedom and personal dignity and worth. . .Poetry, as we have seen, reflected faithfully the desert life. It was the principal form of artistic expression and represented the sum of the community's wisdom and lore as well. Women poets were numerous, and some of them achieved distinction and fame. They participated in the contests at the annual fairs and shared with the poets the festival honors and admiration of the poetry loving crowds.

Many are the wise women whose advice and counsel men sought and acted upon. There were priestesses also, who, in the discharge of their religious functions, enjoyed the reputation of superior knowledge and foresight. . .The Koran speaks of the relationship between man and woman as one of mutual confidence, affection and compassion. . . In those days women were not secluded or veiled but appeared at public functions in the company of men. . .Living for others as she does the Arab woman has achieved the strength and force of character which comes from rising above self and projecting one's life into other lives. Such a concept of self-fulfillment through others has banished restlessness and frustration from her life and given her dignity, serenity and poise."

This latter insight is profound and very relevant. This is why men and women today in the Arab and Muslim world are working together for the realization of their ideals and hopes. And this is why it is not strange that Muslim women who have worked against great odds and survived, are so outstanding and so self-assured.

We remember Turkish men who were sympathetic to the women's movement (which really began in the middle of the nineteenth century). In the foreword of her splendid book, "Moslem Women Enter a New World," an American YWCA secretary, Ruth Frances Woodsmall, summarizes a part of her nine year experience as a secretary in Turkey and Syria:

The transformation of the Near East, especially in Turkey gripped my attention. From the balcony of our residence in Taksim Square witnessing as if from a box seat in a play the main events of the change in Turkey, I realized that I was witnessing the drama of the changing East. The swift sequence of events in Turkey constantly lured me on to seek to know of the meaning of change that lay behind its external evidence and especially to lift the veil in order that I

might catch some glimpse of what was happening in the life
of Moslem women.

Miss Woodsmall, beloved and respected by Turkish women, and Muslim
women in general, did indeed do a great deal to "lift the veil." In more recent
times educators, missionaries and YWCA fraternal workers have made a great
difference in their support of the aspirations and ideals of women. Once in
Istanbul I remember a Turkish gentlemen saying to Miss Phoebe Clary of the
YWCA, "You in the YWCA (Girls Dershane) are the conscience of the
Turkish men." The American mission schools and universities also played a
leading part in the education of Turkish women.

For example, through Turkish friends Miss Clary learned of the plight of
small children forced to live in prison with their mothers. Exposed as they were
to other prisoners, and having little privacy, recreation or stable family life, it is
a wonder they behaved as well as they did. Under these dreadful conditions,
both the mothers and children suffered. The Girls Dershane decided to study
their needs and build a program to help them. The Dershane Board elicited
the advice and help of prominent Turkish women, who made recommenda-
tions for the project.

At first, the prison authorities were somewhat skeptical of these "do-
gooders" as they tend to be in all countries, but when they saw the practical
and helpful potentials of the project they cooperated fully.

The prison granted permission to take the women and children away
from the prison certain days of the week on released time. A balanced program of social recreational and counselling activities was worked out. The Girls
Dershane, using their volunteers as well as professional staff, organized recreation, sewing and music classes, and a day care center which freed the mothers
for a time from care of their children. Also a hot meal was served, giving the
nutrition not available in the prison fare.

The Mens Dershane was asked to provide recreation and games for the
children in its gymnasium. The staff gave overtime services free of charge to
this project.

The response of many in Istanbul to this program was summed up by a
prominent Turkish attorney, "Why didn't somebody think of this before? What
a wonderful program to meet a critical need." Another unexpected result was
that the prison authorities, seeing the improvement in the morale of the
women and children, provided a special place in the prison for mothers and
their children.

ARAB UNITY: FACT OR FANTASY

If there is any one thing that experts on the Arab World agree upon, it is that the Arabic language is probably the leading unifying force in the long history and even the contemporary culture of the people. In recent years the rich Arabic language and poetry are set to music and this moves the Arabs to great deeds in peace and war. One would have thought that their religion, Islam, would be the unifying factor — and it does have a profound influence — but even there the rhetoric of religion is deeply rooted in the experience of the people, whether they are nomads or city dwellers. The Prophet Mohammad, himself a product of the desert, built his appeal around the simple lives of the nomads and worked out his religious philosophy and rules in relation to their needs and their style of living. Another reason why Arabic is a unifying force for the peoples is because it is the means of communication not only for the Muslim but for Christians and Jews and even unbelievers in Arab lands.

Once in Jerusalem, an Arab Christian friend and I stopped in a small shop in the bazaar where a Muslim Arab was manager. As they chattered away in Arabic over tea I could only understand an occasional word, but I observed the rapport that the language created between them. Glancing around the shop, I noticed a wall design with writing in the classical script. On inquiry the shopkeeper said, "How did you know that I have wanted somebody to translate that for a long time? Now, my Arab brother here can do so for us." In the Arab world the language is a bridge, so that wherever Arabs travel in neighboring nations they feel at home when Arabic is spoken.

In his brilliant book, "Arab Unity: Hope and Fulfilment," Dr. Fayez A. Sayegh, an Arab Christian recognized as a scholar throughout the Arab world as well as in the West, stresses the two trends in Arab lands today: one is "static nationalism" implying the status quo; the other is "dynamic nationalism". Dr. Sayegh speaks of dynamic nationalism as one road toward unity among the Arab peoples. Dr. Sayegh is not alone among Arab intellectuals in his emphasis on the will and aspirations of the people.

As a basis and background for his emphasis on the two kinds of nationalism, Fayez Sayegh enunciates two principles: one, that whenever foreign influence over Arab destiny has asserted itself, the result has been Arab political dismemberment; obversely, whenever Arab unification has been accomplished, it has been by Arab will, upon the initiative and at the hands of the Arabs themselves. It follows from these two principles that the progress of the Arab world toward political unification is certain to be directly proportional to the triumph of the "dynamic" brand of nationalization over the "static" type of thinking currently predominant in official circles of many Arab states. The prospects of Arab unity are, therefore, a function of the prospects of dynamic nationalism in Arab society at large.

For another, but rather parallel, point of view I turn to Dr. Nejla Izzeddin's equally brilliant and relevant book, "The Arab World", where she devotes a

chapter to Arab unity. These are her own summaries on the subject:
. . .in the midst of dissension and discord the voice of Arab
unity is clearly and forcefully heard, and the ideal of
recreating a united Arab nation is one of the real forces
which contend for the allegiance of the Arab peoples, an inspiration and a message of hope to a large section of the nation's youth and other representatives of articulate public
opinion. . .The Arabic language is one of the strongest
bonds which hold the Arabs together. . .The modern Arab
renaissance began with the revival of classical Arabic. A
newly Arabicized leader, Ibrahim Pasha, placed the confines
of the Arab countries at the limits where the Arabic language
was spoken. When, during his campaign, which aimed at
the detachment of the Arab provinces from the Ottoman
Empire, Ibrahim Pasha was asked how far he intended to
carry his conquests, he answered, 'As far as the Arabic
language is spoken and as I can communicate with the people in that tongue.'. . .The Arab movement is not an in-
novation, a borrowed concept, or an alien ideology. On the
contrary it is a re-creation of a social order which the Arabs
knew at a time when their society was creative, dynamic
and constructive. It aims at the realization of social solidarity
and political stability, and the reestablishment, through
moral rebirth, of the place and mission of the Arabs in the
family of nations.
When the dream of a just and lasting peace in the Middle East is finally realized, the world may be astonished at the contribution the Arab genius will bring
to the new unity of all people in that part of the world. When people there can
live in dignity and peace perhaps other men and women can do so. Inshallah.
(If God wills.)

The Sûk Cuma or open air "cafeteria"
in Aleppo, 1933.

LIGHTS ON THE MOUNTAIN

"Great things are done not by merely jostling in the street;
Great things are done when men and mountains meet."
Anonymous

The Middle East is like our second home in New Mexico in the southwest part of the United States in one respect: you are scarcely ever out of sight of the mountains. Once in Bursa, a beautiful city in a spectacular setting at the foot of Uludag (Mount Olympus in Asia), a Turkish friend came to our small hotel where we often stayed for food, rest and the wonderful mineral baths. Out of the blue our friend said, "Today I am going to take you up to Mt. Olympus to see something few tourists ever see." Now there are many fine things to see and enjoy in Bursa, the first capital of the Ottoman Empire. There is the Green Mosque, the enormous and very hot Turkish baths, historic places nearby and the beautiful drive from Bursa over mountain ranges to the Sea of Marmara and the Lake of Nicea not to mention two of the seven churches Paul established within a days drive of Bursa. And, if you are really adventuresome the ancient city of Troy is not far away. But we opted for climbing Mt. Olympus and we were not sorry we did.

Olympus in Asia would be a simple task for experienced mountain climbers but the view from the crest is so vast and filled with history and beauty that you feel you are on a mightier mountain. At the top, our friend, Mustafa, took us to a pile of rocks and said, "This is what I wanted to show you." Our disappointment was obvious but Mustafa was resourceful for he added dramatically, "In ancient times, and especially in the times of the Greek Empire this was where couriers built signal fires to send messages which went from one end of the Empire to the other. It was their means of communication. Allah in His mercy has placed enough high mountains in the chain from Corinth to the Holy Land so that one can see signals all the way. Sometimes these signals warned of war, or announced the coronation of a King, Patriarch or Sultan. How they worked out this complex system is a mystery."

We have often thought of those lights on dark mountains carrying their messages across the empire and likened them to the lights in every nation, lit by men and women of faith and wisdom who have served mankind. So, in this closing chapter I am sharing something I have not shared before in writing: my final report of twenty years in the Middle East and the wonderful reply of my YMCA friend, Joel Nystrom, who with others supported the work of the YMCA world-wide. There is a proverb in Arabic, "God is Great; our boats are small." Many times I wished my boat had been larger — larger in vision, in service, in performance and in wisdom — to meet the challenges.

My final report follows:

February 28th, 1962

Mr. Joel E. Nystrom
Executive Secretary
International Committee YMCA
291 Broadway
New York, N.Y.

Dear Joel:

Since my last Administrative Letter (July 30, 1961) we have left the Middle East after 20 years of service in the area, and 15 years of service with the YMCA in Turkey and Lebanon. It has been our privilege to live and work in the area during formative years in the life of the nations; two revolutions and the war in Turkey; the reforms, and vast changes under Ataturk; the revolutionary changes in Egypt and Palestine, the 1958 revolutions in Iraq and Lebanon. All of these political upheavals, and rapid social changes have had their effect on the work of the YMCA, and most have been an opportunity for its growth and influence. The work in Lebanon and Turkey, not only in program services, but in its emergency aspects; refugee services; relief during revolution and war, and rehabilitation after these events.

That the YMCA has had a vital part in these emergency services has gained for it a respect and an image in the community which now enables it to advance in peacetime. One distinguished Arab leader said after the Revolution, "The Lebanese people will never forget how your organization took the lead in crossing the barbed wire to help people on both sides of the 1958 Revolution."

In the Summer of 1958, at the height of the shooting between rebel and government forces in Lebanon, the YMCA opened a Day Camp at its Beach Center on the Mediterranean. In spite of dire predictions that there would be open hostility between boys from the rebel and government territories, not a single incident occurred at the Day Camp, or on the streets enroute. (At that time the rebel forces controlled two-thirds of Beirut.) The city officials were so impressed with this record that they gave a free pass to all Day Campers to go in and out of their neighborhoods.

Turning to Turkey again, in 1943 when there was considerable tension between the Turks and minority groups the American Dershane had just revived a Business Mens' Club, and had opened membership to all in the community. Some of our laymen predicted that there would be trouble among the different nationalities. Among them were Turks, Armenians, Greeks, Americans, Jews and others. It was not long before games and fellowship, brought them together. As one Greek expressed it, "At the YMCA we leave our politics at the door."

While youth in our country may be over-organized, in the Middle East they are under-organized. The usual pattern of clubs is either political or religious. In Beirut there are some 40 Youth Clubs; some are political like the Greek Club, and some along religious lines, like the Jeunes Catholic Club. Even these clubs, which have worthy objectives, do not ordinarily open their membership to outsiders. The Halk Evleri (People's Houses) in Turkey, with cultural, recreational and social activities, are secular, and worthwhile for all ages. They are open to everybody.

A young Armenian in Istanbul joined the YMCA saying, "It is a sad fact, but youth like myself are no longer welcome in some of the Churches of our neighborhood, which are, sometimes, narrow in their point of view on race." One of the great gifts of the YMCA in the Middle East has been its ability to bridge differences. One evidence of this is that the finest Muslim, Protestant, Catholic and Orthodox Clubs are frequently led by YMCA-trained men. Mr. Abbas Farhat, Director of Social Development in Lebanon, has said, "We owe the YMCA a great deal for its training of our leaders."

If agencies like the YMCA and YWCA and the Missions, miss the opportunity to cooperate with indigenous youth movements, then extremist groups will rush in to fill the vacuum. When a Sports Club in a North Lebanese town asked the community to help, the Communists responded by building an enormous clock tower in the public park. When the YMCA was asked to come in and advise, a Communist attending one of the meetings said that they (the Communists) would double any monies given by the YMCA. The Club's President answered, "But the YMCA is giving advice, not money. If your advice is twice as good as theirs we shall accept it."

In a meeting which I addressed in America during furlough from Beirut, one of the listeners inquired, "Could you summarize for us the character and qualities of the Middle Eastern peoples?" For a moment I was stumped, but this was my reply: Perhaps the words which best describe them are lovable, unpredictable, sometimes volcanic, inscrutable, fatalistic, faithful to those whom they trust and like and visionary. Beneath all of their political and social veneer, they are real people, just as sincere and hungry for understanding as people anywhere. In spite of their changeableness and emotionalism, they are deeply loyal to the people and causes they believe in. In spite of their occasional flirtation with extremists systems, they are deeply committed to freedom, and their faith in God.

In this ever-changing, almost always unpredictable, situation the YMCA is called upon to exercise patience and flexibility, wisdom and skill in meeting the real needs, and aspirations of the youth. One of our laymen said to me after a stormy meeting in Beirut, "Porter, you have to be perfect, nothing short of perfect!" Of course, I demurred, for Allah knows how imperfect I am. That YMCA policies and programs have succeeded is evidenced in the fact that no Middle Eastern mob has ever attacked the YMCA Buildings or personnel. But more positively there is evidence among some of the top leaders of the country that they received their first character-training in the Y.

As I leave the Middle East after two decades, I leave not with sadness, but joy, for there have been mountain peaks in experience and in understanding. One mountain peak is to remain in a country long enough to see boys grow up into men, and girls into women, of whom their country can be proud. Another is to see the training of Staff and laymen bear fruit in more dedicated service to the community. A leading Muslim layman in the Turkish Dershane said, "I know that every hour I give the YMCA is a good investment in the future of my country."

The patience, trust and affection experienced with laymen and staff who must often stand between the Movement and community criticism or jealousy is quite remarkable. These men and women are often deeply rooted in their faith, so they take seriously the spiritual aspects of the YMCA, while remaining true to their own faith.

I treasure work with staff members many of whom sacrificed financially and in many other ways to serve. There were years when it was not only unpopular, but dangerous, to be a YMCA Secretary in parts of the Middle East.

During very tense days in Turkey, due entirely to political realities, our staff, made up of Muslims, Jews and Christians, met regularly for devotions and fellowship. We all, of different faiths, took turns leading the meditation, for we were determined to remain togther as God meant us to remain together.

There were values for our family in living abroad during these momentous years. To be among a people of other cultures and races and religions, with other customs and outlooks, with a different pattern of thinking, was most enriching. Always, whatever the differences, there could be a meeting of hearts and minds somewhere, as we in the harried and hurried West find increasingly difficult to achieve.

It is good, then, to have lived in these times, and to have had the privilege of being in the Middle East, so we are grateful to the YMCA and to our friends out there for wanting us, and supporting us in spite of our shortcomings, but liking us as we were. One only regrets those times when our limitations stood in the way of more excellent service, to the people, and especially the youth, whom we still love and admire.

Faithfully yours,

Ezra P. Young

NATIONAL COUNCIL OF THE YOUNG MEN'S CHRISTIAN ASSOCIATIONS
OF THE UNITED STATES OF AMERICA
CORPORATE BODY: NATIONAL BOARD OF YOUNG MEN'S CHRISTIAN ASSOCIATIONS

INTERNATIONAL COMMITTEE OF THE Y.M.C.A.'S OF THE UNITED STATES AND CANADA

March 30, 1962

Mr. Ezra P. Young
YMCA
1528 Locust Street
St. Louis, Missouri

Dear Ezra:

I had not read your final administrative report when I saw you in Kansas City nor your letter of March 4. In fact I read them on the plane returning to New York. Millard and Chuck had already read them.

I would have wanted to tell you in person how much I appreciate the careful and thoughtful analysis which you have given to the period of time in which you represented us in Lebanon and indeed for your references also to Turkey and the whole Arab world. This is a valuable document and includes both personal observations and quotations which we shall be referring to in the years to come. May I ask whether you feel that we should share this final administrative letter with Harry? I believe that he would find both inspiration and some comfort from it.

Again after reading your report I would want to repeat to you and Jessamine our appreciation to you both for the contributions which you have made to the International Committee and to the Lebanon Movement through your sacrificial service at a time of great attention and critical development. While we cannot predict the course of events in Lebanon and the Middle East, the assessment which I would make at the period when you relinquished your responsibilities is that of a turning point and a clearing away of the past debris necessary for the development of the construction of YMCA Movement in Lebanon.

I wish that we might have had more time than the few minutes we had over the coffee cups to talk about both personal and professional matters. Perhaps we can have another session when I shall be with you in St. Louis in May. I wish you every success in your new responsibilities and hope that you will find real satisfaction in working with your colleagues of the St. Louis YMCA and the West Central Area.

Sincerely,

Joel E. Nystrom

JEN:hh

SOME OTHERS
WHO HAVE MADE A DIFFERENCE

In memory are the many visitors whom we entertained during the more than twenty years in the Middle East. One of the most distinguished, and interesting was Dr. John R. Mott for many years a leading layman in the Methodist Church and active YMCA leader who became known later in his career as "Mr. Ecumenicist". When Dr. Mott made his second visit to Istanbul (1950), he had just won the Nobel Price for Peace and in spite of being in his eighties he was spry and alert. He had come to Turkey to visit the YMCAs and leaders and on a special visit with an old friend, the equally distinguished ecumenical Patriarch of the Orthodox Church, His All Holiness Athenagoras. Dr. Mott was received with honor by all whom he met in Turkey.

Dr. Donald Lowrie, Fraternal Secretary to the Paris YMCA, was his companion and intermediary on this famous visit. Mr. Lowrie, a noted scholar in his own right, often found it necessary to play nursemaid to Mr. Mott. One day during their eight day stay in Istanbul Lowrie said to me: "You know how much I love this remarkable man, but could you help me have a free day in the bazaars to indulge in my favorite hobby — icons." Then minutes later in their hotel, Dr. Mott said to me, "You know Lowrie just wears me out. I wonder if you and I could slip away and have a lemonade in that cafe overlooking the Bosphorous. You see, I have a sore tooth, and perhaps we could use that excuse to escape for a few hours." I entered into the conspiracy with both of them; Lowrie had a great time tracking down icons, and Dr. Mott had a wonderful and painless visit with a young Turkish dentist who had studied at Rochester and lived in the YMCA dormitory in that city. After four lemonades, and reams of reminiscenses, Dr. Mott grew mellow and relaxed and they never knew it was all a conspiracy!

One morning Dr. Mott said, "I want to meet the press. Can you set up a conference for me?" Mr. Lowrie gave me a distress signal that made me hesitate to say "yes" to the great man, for he knew that years before, during Dr. Mott's first visit to Turkey, there had been a rather critical review of his visit, but Lowrie did not realize that Turkey had changed a great deal in the interim. Nor did he know that many young journalists trained abroad had a broader view of things. It was arranged. The next afternoon five young men and a young woman, the men all members of the Dershane, appeared for what they thought would be a routine press conference. It turned out to be one of the great encounters in our lifetime.

Dr. Mott was welcomed in traditional eastern fashion and there were a few polite remarks by the Chief of the Press Corps. Then Dr. Mott made a brief (for him!) opening statement about his life, career and philosophy. Afterwards there was a stunned silence, for at the end of his remarks he commended the journalists for being in "one of the great professions of the world, where you can have a profound influence for peace and understanding." Finally, a young man said, "How can a man we have just met know us, and our need for commendation so well? No one has ever spoken so highly of our profession before."

When we opened the conference for reporters' questions, another reporter said, "Who asks questions of a great man like this? Please, sir, just let him speak and we shall take notes." The next morning Dr. Mott made the front page of three daily papers. He called at 7 a.m. and asked me to be at his hotel with translations as soon as possible. It was Sunday. I called a Turkish friend out of bed to help me with the translations and an hour later we were all together over coffee at the Park Hotel. Lowrie, nodding over his coffee from lack of sleep said, "Mott has done it again! He is a man who specializes in the unexpected."

One morning after courtesy calls on Turkish officials, we were invited by the Patriarch of the Orthodox Church to make a trip on the Marmara Sea to the Island of Halki for a visit to the Orthodox Seminary. Enroute, the tall, stately and smiling Patriarch, respected not only by the Greek community in Turkey but also by many of the Turks, stood on the bridge waving to the crowds at each landing and blessing the crowds pressing closer to the little boat. Simultaneously Dr. Mott, not to be outdone, stood on the second bridge waving to the crowd. The next morning papers reported that "the Patriarch of the West and the Patriarch of the East had blessed the crowds to cheering and excitement seldom seen or heard in those waters."

At the Orthodox Seminary there was more excitement as Dr. Mott spoke to the students about his travels and his love for youth. Afterwards, a dignitary of the Church, an Archbishop, kissed Mott's hand and embraced him saying, "thirty-five years ago as a young priest I heard you speak about race, and it changed my attitudes and life, and I want you to know that I have been stirred again by your remarks and your presence with us."

It has been my privilege to know many great men and women here and abroad. A couple who rate very high are Paul and Margaret Anderson who have been friends for many years, first in this country and then in the Middle Eastern countries where Paul was the American Secretary serving as Advisor and Counselor to the YMCA Secretaries assigned to the National YMCAs in that part of the world. Paul Anderson, representing the International Committee of the YMCA, had served in Moscow as private secretary to John R. Mott; and in Paris, as administrator and advisor to the YMCA working mainly with Russian refugees. This modest but brilliant man, equally at home in New York, Paris, Moscow, Athens or Istanbul, has walked with kings but never lost the common touch.

On one of his visits to Turkey during World War II, I can still see him sitting in a quiet corner of a Turkish police station writing one of his notes of wisdom, advice and encouragement to some secretary in the last town visited. He had just come in on the Orient Express from Eastern Europe and we were waiting for the clerk on night duty to awaken so he could clear Paul's papers. I was all for waking the clerk but Paul said "No, maybe he had a rough night, and anyway I have a few more notes to write." With a start the Turk came to and we took care of our business as if nothing had happened. With some chagrin the clerk observed, "You will not tell anybody I went to sleep on the job, will you?" With the warmth under that great intellect, Paul ignored the question and embraced a man who probably will never forget that night.

In recent years, with his mind and step still spry and with Margaret, his companion of many years, Paul Anderson, a leading layman in the Episcopal

Church and a world authority on orthodoxy, makes yearly visits to the Middle East and Russia where his advice and wisdom are sought and respected. But the greater they come the more human they are and we always knew when Paul visited us that the cookie jar should be generously filled with macaroons and that his Turkish Hamam (bath) must be ready for him.

With no thought of a secondary place among those who have made a difference, and in the interest of saving space, the following persons are mentioned:

- Dr. John Davis, Director of UNRWA (United Nations Refugee Works Agency) and Constantin Vlachopolous, Liaison Officer and Director of Relations with the Voluntary Agencies in UNRWA.
- Willard and Christina Jones, Quakers, and Bishop Najib Cuba'in, First Arab Bishop in the Anglican Church. These friends were leaders in the Near East Christian Council Refugee Work for Palestinian Refugees.
- Harriet Hallett, Marjoria Noyce, Dorothy Blotter, and Dr. and Mrs. Loren Shepard. Dr. Shepard was Director of the Admiral Bristol American Hospital in Istanbul. These friends represented the old American Board (Congregational) Mission in Turkey.
- David Dodge, Cleveland Dodge, laymen in the YMCA in Turkey.
- Mr. and Mrs. Herbert Lansdale, Mr. David Creighton, Advisors to the Greek YMCA. Mr. Lansdale also held administrative and advisory positions in the National and International Committees of the YMCA.
- Mr. and Mrs. Leslie Putnam, Laurens and Kate Seelye, Mr. and Mrs. Luther Fowle, and Mr. Afif Shuhibar, laypersons in the YMCA and YWCA national movements throughout the Middle East.
- The Honorable George C. McGhee, Ambassador to Turkey, and Mrs. McGhee.
- The Honorable Rasheet Karami, former Premier of Lebanon.
- The Honorable Alben Barkley, former Senator and Vice President of the United States, and Head of the Congressional Delegation to Turkey to negotiate for an Aid Mission.
- Nahit and Nermin Hamarat, Gregory Vlastos, Rabbi Elmer Burger, former Director of the Council for Judaism.
- General Bull, Norwegian Head of the UN Peace-Keeping Force in Gaza.
- The Honorable Sinan Korle and Mrs. Korle. Mr. Korle is presently with the Turkish Mission to the United Nations.
- Veli Shefik Gizer, Turkish attorney for the Amerikan Dershane, Istanbul.
- Dr. Lutfu Kirdar, former Governor of the Istanbul Vilayet.
- Reverend and Mrs. Alfred Swan, Madison, Wisconsin.
- Dr. and Mrs. Kirtley Mather. Dr. Mather is a distinguished Professor of Geology at Harvard and a leading layman in the international work of the YMCA.
- Reverend and Mrs. Robert H. Tucker and other friends at First Congregational Church, Houston, Texas for their loving care, support and generosity through the years.
- Reverend and Mrs. Francis Rath, Reverend Marja Coons and friends in the Albuquerque, New Mexico Congregational Church for their love and care.
- His All Holiness Patriarch Athenagoras, Head of the Orthodox Church World-Wide.
- Dr. John R. Mott, Methodist and world Statesman; Nobel Prize for Peace, world traveler, friend of youth, YMCA, "Mr. Ecumenicist."

- Dr. and Mrs. Paul B. Anderson, Orthodox Church authority, one-time secretary of YMCA in Russia, Near East YMCA Advisor.
- Bayan Halide Edip Adavar and Adnan Adivar — Pioneers of the Turkish Republic.
- Donald Lowrie, former Advisor, Paris YMCA.
- Mr and Mrs. Middleton Edwards, Istanbul; British merchant, philanthropist; YMCA and YWCA supporters.
- Colonel and Mrs. Cuthbert Binns, former chairman, Turkish Dershane.
- Melvin and Priscilla Zuck, Quakers.
- The Honorable Charles Malik, former Minister of Foreign Affairs, Lebanon.
- Nezahat Nurettin Ege, Turkish educator.
- Basil Photiades, Socony Company, artist, Turkish Dershane layman.
- Monsignor Joseph Ryan, former Director, Catholic Relief for Refugees, Jerusalem.
- John and Sarah Brewer, Houston, Texas.
- Gregory Vlastos, Istanbul; philosopher, lecturer, author, Princeton and McGill Universities.
- Konrad and Ilse Engelmann, Germany and Turkey. Executive in Financial Division of National Council of YMCA, New York City.
- Walter and Fifi Arndt, Professor and authority in Slavic Studies, Dartmouth
- Dr. Kemal Elbirlik, Neurologist, former Istanbul YMCA dormitory resident and friend.
- Afif Shuhibar, Gaza; former Executive Secretary, Tripoli, Lebanon YMCA.
- Mr. and Mrs. Leslie Putnam, former Executive Secretary, Jerusalem, Israel YMCA.
- Haskiye Toledo, accountant, Istanbul Dershane.
- Hamit Efendi, head servant, Istanbul Dershane.
- Reverend and Mrs. Walter Wiley, Pastor, Dutch Chapel, Istanbul.
- Jack and Linda Blake.

A "beehive" village near Aleppo, Syria around 1933.

BIBLIOGRAPHY

Michael M. Alouf. **History of Baalbek.** St. Paul's Press, Narissa, Lebanon, 12th English Edition, 1956.

Edward Atiyah. **The Arabs.** Penguin Books, Breat Britain, 1958.

Ali Sami Boyar. "Paintings of Aya Sofya". Art folder.

Elmer Berger. **Judaism or Jewish Nationalism.** Bookman Associates, New York, 1957.

John Kingsley Birge. "Secularism in Turkey and its Meanings". **International Review of Missions. London, October 1944.**

John Kingsley Birge. A Guide to Turkish Area Studies. The American Council of Learned Societies, William Byrd Press, Inc., Richmond, Virginia, 1949.

Suleyman Chelebi. Lyman MacCallum and John Murray, translators. "The Mevlidi Sherif" (Birthsong of the Prophet). Albermarle, St. London W., 1943.

Bruce Conde. **See Lebanon.** Harb Bijani Press, Beirut, Lebanon, 1960.

Selma Ekrem. **Turkey, Old and New.** Charles Scribners Sons, New York, 1947.

Funk & Wagnalls, editors. **Brittanic World Language Dictionary.** Encyclopedia Brittanica, Inc., Chicago, 1959.

Harry N. Howard. **The Partition of Turkey — A Diplomatic History, 1913 — 1923.** University of Oklahoma Press, Norman, Oklahoma, 1931.

Nejla Izzeddin. **The Arab World.** Henry Regnery Co., Chicago, 1953.

Evelyn Lyle Kalchas. "Breakfast in Asia and Lunch in Europe". **Life on the Bosphorous.** Matbaasi Press, Bilgehan, 1977.

Alice Geer Kelsey. **Once the Hoja.** Longmans Green & Co., New York, 1943.

Harold Lamb. **Suleiman the Magnificent.** Doubleday & Co., Inc., Garden City, New York, 1951.

Ernest Mamboury. "Constantinople". **A Tourist Guide.** Rizzo and Son, Constantinople, Turkey, 1924.

A. Vahid Moran. **Turkish-English Dictionary.** Turkish Ministry of Education, 1945.

Douglas Chandler. "The Transformation of Turkey". **National Geographic Society.** January, 1939.

Bernard F. Rogers, Jr. "Old Pattern and New In Turkey". **National Geographic Society.** January, 1939.

John Scofield. "Jerusalem, the Divided City". **National Geographic Society.** April 1959.

Thomas J. Abercrombie. "The Sword and the Sermon, An American Muslim Explores the Arab Past". **National Geographic Society.** July 1972.

Pardoe. "Beauties of the Bosphorous". Virtue Magazine. London.

James W. Redhouse. Revised Redhouse Dictionary, English to Turkish. The American Board Publications Department, 1950.

Anwar Sadat. **In Search of Identity, An Autobiography.** Harper & Row Publishers, Inc., 1977-78.

Fayez A. Sayegh. **Arab Unity — Hope and Fulfilment.** The Dev-Adair Company, New York, 1958.

Soubhi Saouaf. George F. Miller, translator. **Aleppo Past and Present.** Ecole Professionelle, G. Salem, Aleppo, Syria, 1958.

Alice C. Shepard. **Shepard of Aintab.** Interchurch Press, 1920.

Desmond Stewart. **The Arab World.** The Life World Library, Time Incorporated, New York, 1962.

Tracy Strong. **A Pilgrimage Into the World of Islam.** World Alliance of Young Mens Christian Associations, Geneva, 1959-59.

Turkish Information Office. **Turkey.** Turkish Information Office, 444 West 52nd Street, New York, Kennerly Press, Inc., 1948.

Frances W. Woodsmall. **Moslem Women Enter a New World.** Round Table Press, Inc., New York, 1936.

Walter Livingstone Wright. **Ottoman Statecraft — The Book of Counsel for Viziers and Governors of Sari Mehmet Pasha, the Defterdar.** 1935.

Ezra Young and Herman Kreider. "Ancient Aleppo". **Travel Magazine.** Robert M. McBride & Company, Inc., March, 1935.

A "town and country" conference in Aleppo in 1933.
(Note the hubble-bubble pipe.)

www.ingramcontent.com/pod-product-compliance
Lightning Source LLC
LaVergne TN
LVHW091225080426
835509LV00009B/1179